About the Author

Nina B. Lichtenstein is a native of Oslo, Norway and holds a PhD in French from the University of Connecticut and an MFA in creative nonfiction from Southern Maine University's Stonecoast program. She is the founder and director of Maine Writers Studio, and the author of *Sephardic Women's Voices: Out of North Africa*. She has three grown sons and lives in Maine with her husband.

ninalichtenstein.com

Praise

"This is a brilliant new way to write a memoir... I feel enriched, and grateful to discover a different way to go through my days. I loved every word."
Abigail Thomas, author of *A Three Dog Life*

"At a time when women's bodies are under more outside scrutiny than ever, it's a joy and a journey to consider our bodies from the inside, and our place in the world through our corporeal selves."
Allison K Williams, author of *Seven Drafts*

"Body as portal, body as record-keeper, body as witness, body as accomplice... *Body: My Life in Parts* eloquently proves that the 'body nation' is a treasure chest of memories waiting for each of us to unlock and explore... A very interesting and provocative read... truly inspiring."
Lesléa Newman, author of *I Carry My Mother*

"This book, like the female body, is full of soft curves and sharp edges, vulnerabilities and scars, impressions and depressions, pleasures and pain... It is muscle memory in the written form. A must read for anyone with a body."
Talya Jankovits, author of *Girl Woman Wife Mother*

"Nina B. Lichtenstein is an archeologist of her own history in these pages, excavating the stories her body holds, bringing them to light. This is a clear-eyed memoir, a book both muscular and graceful, visceral and wise."
Gayle Brandeis, author of
Drawing Breath: Essays on Writing, the Body, and Loss

Body: My Life in Parts

Nina B. Lichtenstein

www.vineleavespress.com

For Tobias, Gabriel, and Benyamin

Author's Note

Events in this book were recreated in good faith and to the best of my ability, subject, as is always the case, to the vagaries of memory. Names and identifying characteristics of some individuals have been changed, to protect their privacy. Conversations and dialogues are re-created from memory, but many phrases are "as spoken" because they are so memorable to me."

I think bodies are about the coolest thing in … ever. Your body. Mine. All the different kinds. What a glory bodies are.

Lidia Yuknavitch

The amount of sensory material stored up or stored down in the brain's and the body's systems is inestimable. It's like a culture at the bottom of a jar, although it doesn't grow, I think, or help anything else to grow unless you find a way to reach it and touch it.

Seamus Heaney

Prologue

It's humbling to wake up in the middle of the night and realize your life is more than halfway to "the end" and that *AARP Magazine* is written for you. A couple of summers ago, when I got up for the now-predicable middle-of-the-night bathroom run, I noticed a shooting pain in my right hip, and took a few tentative steps. Through quiet groans, I hobbled on despite the sharp jabs. While I sat on the toilet, my mind raced. What was this pain about? Could it be that I overexerted myself in yesterday's morning yoga flow? Or is it those damn excess twenty (thirty?) pounds I've been lugging around since menopause, fucking me over? Worse yet, could it be cancer? *Oh my god, here it is: it's coming for me.* I had just lost a friend to the silent killer that is ovarian cancer and knew this destroyer of lives causes pain anywhere *but* in the ovaries.

As I limped back to bed in the dark, I thought, why not write about the memories lodged within my various body parts? *Before it's too late,* my morbid internal voice chimed in. I wanted to understand how I've gotten to this past-the-midpoint in life, and I imagined my body would be the most reliable record-keeper. In that moment, I felt an urgent intimacy and need for complicity with my body to make sense of it all. *Use me to account for your story*, it whispered. *Eyes, breasts, hips, and feet: they will collaborate with you and guide your remembrances*, it promised.

I'm a front-end Gen-Xer, but born in 1965, I am also a tail-end Baby Boomer. I live suspended between the two generations, avoiding a peg hole both by dint of my vintage, and my unusual identity as an expat Norwegian Lutheran turned American Viking Jewess. I and most of my generation are suddenly in our mid to late fifties, no longer blissfully unaware of the challenges that aging brings. My body-awareness sings to a different tune, now, that I'm no longer in my thirties or forties or even early fifties. It's impossible to ignore body parts like the achy knee, the difficulty reading the fine print, or the greying hair, and let's not mention the unapologetic southbound direction of my breasts and the brazen horizontal expansion of my hips and belly—and I realize how utterly thankful I am for each day that passes without too much corporeal drama. I still appreciate the relatively peaceful conduct of my limbs, organs, and parts—the ones that continue to work well, those that need a little extra TLC, and the loyal survivors that have been out to battle but still hang on, persistent in their commitment to not jump a decidedly sinking ship.

That night when my hip was killing me, I fumbled for the pen I try to leave on my night table exactly for moments like these, when an idea enters my mind but can vanish just as quickly. Jotting it down, I can recall it in the morning, when I am alert and ready to explore our compatibility. Thus, this project was born.

My body, which promised to guide me on this journey, became a portal for the remembering and recording of scars and blessings, traumas and joys, shame and pride, even the smallest moments long forgotten; all experiences lodged deep within the body parts' unique shapes, tissue, fascia, and nerve-endings because the body is at once witness and accomplice, reliably present when sometimes—perhaps often— the mind is not. Each body part is a treasure chest waiting to have its lock picked and content discovered and examined, touched again, felt again, and maybe even understood from the point of view of the person I've become. What happened in and to the body of this woman, daughter, mother, wife, lover, friend, teacher, writer, and how do all these bodily life-moments become the building blocks of "me?"

It's the generative partnership between body and mind I explore in these pages, as body parts get a turn in the driver's seat to steer me toward remembering. The mind, on its end, does what co-pilots are good at: planning the journey and making sure we reach our endpoint, which in truth is not an end with a point at all, but rather a *process* of discovery. Think of it as a way to feel grounded by the often-elusive gift of the memory of experience, channeled through the pure physicality of flesh, bones, nerves, and cells. Combined with the kind of examination that can help us come to terms with a past that is always, already, carried in the body, this physically anchored, explorative adventure allows us to take ownership of the role as creator of our own life and our own stories.

Let's imagine that to *re-member*—to bring together a body of disparate memories—is an attempt to gather and make whole that which has been dis-membered, broken, or forgotten. The shape of *Body: My Life in Parts* resonates with how our memories are formed: by interconnected fragments that communicate with one another, build upon one another, and collaborate to enable a sense-making journey. And there is quite a bit of what I'll call cross-pollination: as I examine one body part that unlocks a door to a room containing certain sensory or emotional memories, other doors tend to swing open all by themselves, like a domino effect. Unexpectedly, a new cache of remembrances reveals itself that may at first seem unrelated to the original body part. All this to say, as you read on (or explore your own body memories), expect the unexpected: the body may have physical limitations, but the mind does not. In cahoots, the two can generate a flow that reveals the breathtaking interconnectedness of the life events and their memories that make each of us uniquely singular. This is our shared experience, what it means to be alive.

It is my hope that when you read this book, it may not so much inform you about me and my life specifically, but rather, show you how generative it can be to mine our body parts and in the end that you may consider how your own life-memories are embedded in *your* body parts. I'd like to imagine that while you read about (my) knees, or (my) ears or (my) belly, you'll feel compelled to turn your gaze and mindfulness inwards and prod your own body for what memories it holds for you. Be open, ask it to speak to you, and listen closely. You can check out the back pages of this book for a variety of body memory prompts to get you started on your own journey of discovery.

Eyes

It's not what you look at, it's what you see.
Henry David Thoreau

My best friend Anne, whom I grew up with in Oslo and whom I've known since first grade, always reminds me I have what she calls "sorry eyes." I know exactly what she means because I can see it and recognize that melancholy look, even when I am neither blue nor happy, but just neutral in mood. Ever since I was a teen, people have told me I look like the Norwegian actress Liv Ullmann. She has big-time sorry eyes, too, reminiscent of a basset hound's sad expression.

I used to hate the idea that I might resemble Liv Ullmann, because she was known for the gloomy and depressed characters she portrayed. Her ex-husband, the iconic film director Ingmar Bergman, knew how to work with her downhearted aura in her early film successes like *The Emigrants* (1971) and *Scenes from a Marriage* (1973). But the fact that I didn't like being told I resembled Norway's most well-known actress sticks deeper than looks. Liv's daughter, Linn, went to the same elementary and middle school as Anne and I, and she also lived on our street with her mother and Mrs. Moe, their housekeeper. Linn was possessive of Anne and came between us. I felt that I couldn't compete, since Linn and her mother led what I thought was a glamorous lifestyle, inviting Anne to join them in exotic and faraway locations like New York City, Italy, and the Caribbean. When we'd hang out or have playdates, I was the third wheel. Not seen, it was as if I didn't exist.

One incident stands out. Three lanky middle schoolers, we were in Linn and Liv's sprawling Oslo apartment with high ceilings and huge rooms connected by generous archways. They even had a fireplace in the kitchen and a sauna in the far end of a lushly carpeted hallway that went on forever. Linn took Anne into her bedroom to play and locked the door, while I was left in the dark and quiet hallway. I think I cried, or at least moped, as I wandered down the hall. When I got to the living room, I discovered Liv sitting on the sofa. I knew she was famous, so the moment I spotted her had some of that "should I even look at her" hesitation. I peeked timidly in her direction. Was she smoking a cigarette? In my mind's eye, I see an oversized, rust-colored corduroy sectional, and a 1970s floor lamp craning its long, stainless-steel neck over a low, square, marble coffee table. A large, round, white glass globe is suspended midair, a moon within reach. The star sat below the moon, shrouded in a cloud of smoke.

"Hello there," a gentle voice said.

"Hi," I said, hyper aware that a real-live celebrity was addressing me. She was enigmatic to me because she seemed like such a regular person there, on the couch. I also didn't understand how she was so legendary when all I had heard was my parents talk about how they didn't think she was a good actress, and that they found Bergman's films dark and depressing. My parents were looking for entertainment, not films without satisfying endings about complex, gloomy lives.

"You seem a bit unhappy, what's going on?" she asked.

"They locked the door and won't let me in," I answered, feeling weird about telling on them.

"Don't care about them," she said. "You can sit here with me and ignore how they are behaving." She smiled at me with her forlorn eyes that only intensified my self-pity, but it also felt good to be noticed by somebody, and not just anybody.

I plopped down on the far side of the couch, stealing furtive glances at the star, then gazed around the spacious room. Large and colorful abstract oil paintings adorned the walls, nothing like the small paintings and prints we had at home. There might have been a glass of juice, or maybe I was even offered a soda. I was used to second-hand cigarette smoke from home, so while hers may have drifted slowly around our heads, trailing like a mysterious, floating blanket, it would not have bothered me. Perhaps we just sat there in silence, me feeling awkward but relevant because I had been invited in, to a sort of communion.

As rejected and invisible as Linn and Anne made me feel, the intimacy Liv offered by letting me sit so casually close to her, turned the experience from one of agonizing, adolescent ache into a memory of, I think I'd like to call it *redemption*. I wasn't alone or scorned, but instead joined and *seen* in my isolation by someone kind who accepted me and maybe even understood me—a famous person to boot!

Like Liv Ullmann, I have blue eyes, blond eyebrows and eyelashes, as well as high Nordic cheekbones. I see our shared features better now that I am an adult. As an adolescent girl, I didn't think Liv was beautiful, and I wonder how much of my opinion about her was shaped by overhearing my parents' critique of her talent, and of my feelings toward her daughter for stealing my best friend.

Today, I look at photos of the young Liv Ullmann, posing with Ingmar Bergman and Linn, their scrawny towheaded girl, and I think, *gosh, Liv was so beautiful.* Ullmann's beauty revealed itself to me as I matured, and it's quite possible it was her compassion that day in the 1970s that was the beginning of this evolution in what I see when I look at her image today.

Perhaps what planted itself as an early experience of kindness took hold and grew into my own personal conviction of how important it is to validate the other's presence by truly seeing and acknowledging her, not just looking. Ullman *saw* me in a moment when I felt unseen, and this in turn validated my being. My body remembers *this moment.*

Not only did my first pair of glasses help thirteen-year-old me see better, but more importantly they made me think people saw me as more mature and distinguished. During a routine annual check-up at my middle-school doctor's office it was established I was farsighted and should have reading glasses (Norwegian public schools had doctor and dentist offices on site, thanks to socialized medicine.) Off I went with my mom or dad to the optometrist downtown, where I tried on dozens of different shapes, until I finally decided on the frame I liked best: Aviator shaped and tortoise colored; it was the late 1970s after all. The waiting period before we could pick up my new spectacles seemed forever. Meanwhile, I anticipated how they would change my life, how they would make me feel special. When the day came to pick them up and I put them on, I didn't like how they made the world seem unstable, and I felt dizzy and nauseous when I wore them. At home, I put them in the top drawer of the small, wooden desk in my room, the same desk my mom had used as a child, and where I did my homework and wrote in my journal.

I didn't wear my glasses often; every now and then, I would put them on while I did homework. But most of the time I would just slide the drawer of my desk open, touch the soft, black case that held them, maybe peek inside as if to check the glasses hadn't disappeared, and then close the drawer again. Eventually, I got used to their prescription and the world returned to a more stable version of itself when I wore them. Sometimes, I'd bring them to school, though wearing them made me painfully self-conscious, and it was also a hassle to put them on and take them off for recess and to see the blackboard. I'd misplace them or forget them at home. It was an erratic affair, but something happened to my experience of myself each time I put the glasses on. I imagined myself more bookish than I was, rarely reading outside of schoolwork and only having had a short-lived love-affair with Nancy Drew and the Hardy Boys. I didn't have any concept of what an intellectual was, or that there even was such a thing, but a palpable sensation of wisdom and import beyond my years came over me when the plastic frames rested on my nose.

I recently found my first pair of glasses in a box of keepsakes from childhood that my mother mailed me from Norway when she was in one of her clearing-the-storage-space moods. The glass in the frames was dusty and the plastic tortoise finish had lost its luster. There were tiny bite marks on the tip of the right temple, which made me smile. The first thing that struck me was how small the glasses were. They were the first in a long string of eyeglasses in all shapes, sizes, and colors that I have had throughout my life. There were the green retro wingtips; the red rounded ones; the purple metal rectangles with magnetic Snap-On shades; the round, wire-rimmed ones; and the current grey, large, squarish frames that cost way too much. The excuse? I had just gone through menopause and thought, *fuck it, if not now, when? I deserve these.*

Today I have progressive lenses because that's what happens with age, and I am no longer farsighted, but need glasses for distance and must take them off for reading. It's funny, because I never considered that maybe one reason why I didn't like to read when I was young was because I needed glasses. Looking back, I always attributed my tomboyish behavior and penchant for outdoor action, as opposed to the indoor, sedentary and quiet act of reading, to my difficulty with attention. More on this later, in the "Brain, Mouth, Butt" chapter, where I explore my conspiracy theory regarding this bodily trio and its role in my so far self-diagnosed ADHD.

·

When I consider my eyes, and the act of seeing or being seen, another memory surfaces: that moment you notice out of the corner of your eye that you are watched by someone and judged.

My ten-year-old knees have scratches, my shins are full of bruises in shades of blue and green, and a house key dangles on a string around my neck. I'm climbing the sprawling lilac tree outside the entrance to our apartment building because there's a small, round bird's nest perched between two branches about two-thirds of the way up, and I'm curious. I want to see the creatures that belong to the tiny, frantic, v-shaped beaks that bob above the nest's edge. When my foot has a solid hold on a cross branch below, I crane my neck and gape at three miniscule, purple chicks with skin so thin and barely formed, their miniature, plump blood vessels pulsate through its shimmery surface.

I reach into the delicate, round basket built of reedy straw and twigs and touch the warm, delicate hatchlings. They don't see me because their eyes are still sealed shut in strange bulges smaller than lentils, facing skyward. But they are quiet now, and huddle together, their little orange bills closed. I gently grab one of the chicks, the desire to measure its weight and feel its budding life in my hand stronger than my sense of wrongdoing, and then it happens. The chick wiggles and falls to the ground.

As I scamper down from the tree to pick it up, one of our neighbors, the old bachelor Mr. Selmer Andersen, who gives me saltine crackers and apple juice in his apartment, and who has fancy leather club chairs and lampshades made of translucent animal skin stitched together with what I imagine is sinew, exits our building. He looks at me, and then his eyes trail to the grass beneath me where the purple, featherless lump lies.

He makes a fist as he locks eyes with mine and shakes his head, his normally kind face now stern under crinkled, bushy eyebrows. He says nothing, but he has said everything. I see and am seen. To this day, that little girl is still in me; caught and exposed as mischievous and careless, judged even, in one of my very own origin-story sins.

·

When my three sons—Tobi, Gabi, and Benya—were young, say seven, five, and four, they thought I had magic eyes in the back of my head. This they believed because I told them so.

"Hold your horses, little guy, where do you think you are going with that?" I'd confront one of them if I caught him sneaking off with a Fig Newton or his brother's Gameboy or a Juicy Juice box. The kid would look at me with big eyes, wondering how in the world I knew what was hidden behind his back or in his pocket or under his t-shirt.

"What do you mean?" he'd say, trying to look all innocent, gaze wandering aimlessly around the room, avoiding the eye contact that risked revealing the offense.

"Mamma has eyes in the back of her head, don't you know that?" I'd say, drilling my stare deeper into my naughty boychik's puss. "I can see *everything*."

A look of incredulity and a crooked smile flashed across the culprit's face.

"Really, Mamma?"

"Really."

"Can I see them?" he'd try to outsmart me. "The extra eyes, show them to me!"

"Nope. When I don't need them, they retract into my neck" I said, using a fancy word and hoping the kid would leave it at that.

"Nooo, c'mon Mamma, it's not true!" he'd try.

"Oh, it's true alright," I'd say, turning away to feign that I was done with the discussion.

I could sense his stare on the back of my head, looking for his mother's magical eyes that got him into trouble.

"Now, put back that Fig Newton where you found it, or at least, ask permission before you just go and take it," I'd say, to finalize the matter.

There'd be a giggle or a sigh, followed by "Can I *please* have a Figguh Newton, Mamma?"

"Yes, you may. But bring your brothers one each also, and remember to ask before you take next time, okay munchkin?"

"Okay, Mamma," he'd say with a satisfied smile and scamper off.

And the myth lived on for a few more years; they saw me as being the holder of quite a few Mamma-superpowers. I relished being seen this way by my munchkins.

But, as the boys grew, the sham of their mother's extra set of eyes was eventually exposed, and they came to see me as somewhat superhuman thanks to other prodigious skills I showcased for them and their friends. I built the best snow forts (thanks to my Norwegian winter games genes), made awesome Norwegian waffles (served warm with butter and sugar, it's their sweet heart shape and the cardamom in the batter that makes them unforgettable), and raced them down ski-mountains with glee. It was a rough day when I realized they'd beat me down the slopes.

The older they got, the more mortal and flawed I became. They eventually realized the undeniable truth: I wasn't invincible, and my only superpower was my ability to love them no matter what. My view of them changed as well, from that of clumsy wolf-cubs who needed their mama, to a lithe pack of ferociously protective man-wolves, intuitively intuned to their mother's well-being. Now that they are adults, they envelop me with emotional generosity and seem to see me as though I'm the fragile one, the one that needs her boys' well-developed superpowers (genetic, right?) in loving affection to keep her safe and happy. Somehow, the roles are reversing; today it's me who gawks at them and finds them magical in every which way.

.

The idea of observing scenes, events, or thoughts as they occur without judgment and without reacting is a relatively recent notion for me. My favorite yogi, Omkara, repeatedly reiterates the value of "just observing without judgment" during our yoga and meditation practice. My therapist, Scott, also echoes a version of this. "Be aware of the reactivity," he warns and encourages me to pause and take a few mindful breaths whenever I feel triggered. "Just notice before you react," he says.

It seems that I'm finally able to internalize and put to good practice this mindfulness of clarity of vision. After years of yoga, mindfulness, and meditation practice; and years of couple's and individual therapy, I am beginning to see, that is *understand*, that I have lived a life full of reactivity. Until recently, it has not been natural for me to not judge, to not react. This unfortunate impulse has led to much unnecessary suffering. Perhaps also some comic relief and outlandish behaviors that friends and family see as either mildly entertaining or annoying, but more than anything, it has caused agitation and weightiness between others and myself, as well as in my own core.

One palpable fringe benefit of patient observing (vs. reacting) is that something magical happens. First, I must focus on my breath. Turning my full attention to my breathing enables me to remain free from judgmental or opinionated thoughts, or worse, from impulsive reactions that only prolong disquiet. The magic is that when I manage to follow my yogi's and therapist's advice, I am detached in that moment from whatever is not pure breath. That does not mean I don't notice things, but that a burden is lifted, which in turn gives a welcome and true sense of release.

If I think about how my life might have been different had I understood and practiced this concept, say, twenty years ago, or even ten years ago, it almost takes my breath away.

At fifty-seven, I can say with confidence that my over-five-decades of life experience has helped me gain valuable insight, thank goodness—one clear benefit of aging. In yoga, this connection to wisdom is attributed to the third eye chakra, a kind of symbolic gateway of connectedness to self. Located on the forehead, between the eyes, this mindful portal leads to the inner realms and spaces of higher consciousness, allowing access to the kind of unfettered guidance that comes from deep within our being, a sort of visual intuition. Who knew turning the gaze inward as opposed to outward is what true vision is really about?

My body is aging, and gravity is taking its toll, but with the mindful shift in perspective through the third eye comes a lightness of being which I think can carry me onward.

That is what I see now.

Breasts

I make milk. What's your superpower?
Unknown

I gave birth to three sons in four years and breastfed one after the other. I essentially had three in diapers at the same time because my oldest just wouldn't shit on the potty even though he was four. It took my husband Dan and me several years to get pregnant the first time, and it wasn't until after some fertility work and a cycle of hormone-boosting shots in the butt that the little embryo that was to become our first-born finally stuck and grew to a solid nine-pound four-ounce Viking Jew baby. After Tobi's birth, or Tobias Thor as he was aptly named, we felt we didn't have the luxury to plan a pregnancy and birthing schedule, so we just agreed to accept what happened next. Two more happened quickly. Busy days and years followed. I was up to my elbows in poop, and the level of bodily exhaustion made stuff that wasn't relevant to daily survival fall by the wayside. Pages of baby books that had been offered as gifts remained mostly blank, despite the half-written sentences that we just had to fill in:

The first word you surprised us with was ____________.

We were so excited the day we saw your first tooth:
___/___/______.

Of course, there were lots of teeth and words and steps, but no specifics remain in my memory. It was painful to find the leather-bound artisanal baby books with the little silver charms attached to a blue ribbon on the front covers, tucked away in storage when I got divorced and was packing to move out of the house. The thick, papyrus, cream-colored pages were empty, save for each child's name written in ink on the first page: This book belongs to Tobias Thor. Gabriel Balder. Benyamin Odin.

Tobi nursed the longest. No disruptions or competition for attention from siblings, he and I enjoyed this profound and privileged intimacy for about nine months. Eventually, our before-bedtime nursing moments were more for the cozy snuggle session than for feeding, and in time those came to a natural end. The sensation of the milk letdown is viscerally vivid still: that tingling, stinging feeling around thirty seconds after the baby latched on and sucked, as the milk began to flow. Sometimes the milk came so fast and with such abundance that the little one didn't have time to keep up and would choke and cough, at which point I would have to press down on my nipple to prevent the stream of milk from continuing squirting, spraying his face, until he was ready to latch on again. Other times, he just let the excess bluish-white and sweet liquid run out from the side of his mouth, his eyes fixed on mine.

The intimacy during nursing is like no other inter-human experience I've ever lived, our faces fewer than twelve inches apart, our senses hyper-focused on one another. My baby's sweet smell, his hair and skin and cute cotton rompers. His tiniest movements and sounds, the way his little feet would occasionally kick or jerk if he nodded off in the middle of nursing, and the sounds of hungry gulps or fulfilled burps. His body warm, pulled close to mine, and his rhythmically moving lips and tongue enveloping my nipple with an innocent greed, soft and warm and confident, surprising each time. I have not gazed or been gazed at in this primal way since.

Gabriel, or Gabi, born two weeks shy of two years after Tobi and weighing in at eleven pounds, twelve ounces (!) was much more sensitive, thus more easily distracted as a baby, and nursing him was often interrupted by his brother's needs and sheer presence. After about six months, Gabi was too worried he was missing any action in the world around him, and twisted and squirmed as I put him to my breast. It soon stopped making any sense insisting or trying. Then, less than eighteen months after Gabi was born, when he was still just a little dude trying to figure out how to stake his own ground in our family order, the surprise of Benyamin, aka Benya, arrived, and poor Gabi didn't know what hit him. Benya sabotaged forever Gabi's idea and opinion of our priorities as parents—a dynamic that has influenced our family ever since.

To this day, Gabi is more hyper-alert about the fairness of things and is emotionally triggered more easily than his brothers; to this day I still feel—from both his end and mine—an acute awareness of our shared sensitivity and need for connection, perhaps a connection that was interloped by his new brother; to this day, as he approaches thirty and I sixty, I notice —not without some self-criticism—that I seem to give him more attention than his brothers, as if I have a subconscious need to continue to nurture him (breasts, remember?) and make up for the surprise ambush of Benya. I want (need?)

to assure Gabi (and myself?) there will always be room for him in my ability to mother, even though, or perhaps especially because, he was squeezed in the middle as a wee one. Maybe I'm trying to make up for how crazy those early years were, how little time and energy I had for him then, and it could be I'll always be (subconsciously) compensating for his emotional needs I was unable to meet at the intense time of my breastfeeding years.

His older and younger brothers remain more unruffled and easygoing, and don't care so much or even pay attention to equality as much as comfort (or, discomfort). Contrary to Gabi's (and my?) urge to stay in touch more frequently, often daily and about the minutia and dilemmas of daily living, the brothers and I speak and text more sporadically. I often wonder what we did differently in raising the boys, since at the time, I had no awareness of differentiating between them. But of course, I did, because nothing can be the same with three unique personalities. As time passed and family interplays embedded themselves into habitual patterns, we were all taking part in cementing the sometimes complex, sometimes beautiful dynamics of our family story.

Benya was born a laid-back person who, from the get-go, knew what he wanted, made little fuss about getting it, and figured out how to solve situations in a quietly independent manner ever since he was a toddler. That was his way of navigating the same system that made his eighteen-months-older brother Gabi an often hilarious, but clingy and anxious, little monkey. Of course, we *think* it was the same system, but in reality, each child would have his uniquely individual family experience, and we our distinct parenting journeys.

Benya enjoyed nursing, too, my breasts an open buffet replenished on demand, and he gained weight the way he should. He was, like his brothers, in the ninety-fifth percentile of the growth chart at every check-up with their pediatrician, whose "ohhhs and ahhs" and marveling filled the examining room. I relished the nursing time spent with Benya, belly to belly, gently pressed toward my bosom, in a more mindful way, mournful even, knowing from experience the looming end of this cherished bonding ritual. And to that end, Benya's modus operandi of having his own very specific ideas about how to do things, snuck up on me unexpectedly.

My fellow ex-pat and Israeli girlfriend Yosefa and I raised our kids in the same town—one street apart—and together had long planned a weekend together in New York City. Two exhausted mothers hoping for a boost of energy and some alone-time away from our needy toddlers, we'd schemed about the cultural venues we'd visit and what newly prized culinary hot spots to include in our two-day "mamas on the town" extravaganza. I pumped breast milk in between nursing for weeks, storing sealed baggies in the freezer, so that the able-bodied rotating child-care trifecta of my husband, mother in-law, and babysitter could step into my place as substitute wet-nurses.

My weekend bag was stuffed with breast pump parapher-nalia that took up more space than my clothes and toiletries combined. I kissed all my boychiks goodbye—the three little ones as well as their dad—and off we girls went on our first non-baby weekend in as long as we could recall. Since my milk production had increased heartily due to the pumping I had done in addition to the regular nursing, I would have to keep extracting breast milk while away in order to slowly scale back to Benya's twice-a-day morning-and-night routine. So, I whipped out my little handy-dandy manual breast pump in the bathroom stalls of the MoMa, the Guggenheim, and at the Eugene O'Neill Theater on 49th Street. God knows what other patrons thought I was doing in the stall where I was taking my time, sweating and fumbling while the bathroom line moved swiftly in and out of all the other stalls. I'd dump the breast milk I extracted in the toilet before leaving the little enclosure, guilty about all the babies in the world who could use it.

Yosefa and I took an early afternoon train home on Sunday, for me to arrive in time for Benya's evening nursing. Calls were made on the way home to ensure perfect timing; that my baby would be ready in his PJ's but not given a bottle so he would be eager for his meal, this time directly from the mother-source. My breasts were about to burst; they were engorged and tender, full of milk ready to be guzzled down by my ravenous wee one. I arrived home just before 7 p.m., and Tobi and Gabi jumped all over me, excited for presents and treats. Benya came crawling on all fours, mellow as always and ready for bed in his yellow-and-blue striped one-piece pajamas.

After I hugged and kissed his older brothers, handing them each a campy New York City souvenir—a yellow wind-up cab with doors and trunk that opened, a statue of liberty whose crown lit up in bright colors—I swept Benya into my arms and headed upstairs for his bedroom, where our favorite rocking chair sat in the dark corner, a baby-blue patchwork quilt draped over the back, and a padded footstool ready in front. This was a quiet part of the house, far away from the noisy, animated brothers and our two yapping Lhasa Apso dogs, Yoffie and Shooggie. It was a perfect place to settle down, for Benya, and for me, wired as I was after two nights in the city that never sleeps.

I pulled up my shirt and took a hold of my baby's body the way I always did when nursing, his arm fitting snugly behind my ribs and his belly facing mine, his face nuzzled against my chest.

After a few quick sips he let go of my nipple and twisted toward the closed door to his room, the light from the hallway visible in a slim stream beneath the bottom, faint sounds travelling from downstairs where all the action was taking place with new toys and our lively puppies.

I pulled him gently toward me, but he arched his back and resisted. I pulled more, coaxing him along. "Come on little guy, look what Mamma has for you! Yumm!"

His eyes caught mine briefly, as if pacifying me with his own message saying, "Relax Mamma, I love you and all that, but I'm just not too into this anymore," before he again arched his back and squirmed, twisting his upper body away from me, toward the door, the light, the sounds, the action.

"Come on, honey," I heard myself utter, and when I realized it wasn't going to happen, I mumbled, "You've got to be kidding me." I took a deep breath and tried to relax my shoulders that had tensed up. I tried to not force anything, fearing he might sense my desperation. "You're done? That's it?" I looked at his face. A steady drip of milk wet my shirt and the soft, cloth diaper under his chin, while he listened intently for the activity outside his room, eyes wide as if this improved his ability to hear his brothers better, completely uninterested in me. I stopped trying to lure him back.

I was not prepared for the timing of this final separation,

and I rested my head back in the dark, the weight of Benya in my lap, my breast bare and cold without the warmth of his mouth and cheeks against my skin.

We sat like this for a few minutes, and eventually milk stopped trickling. I carried him downstairs and told Dan what had happened. When I sat Benya down on the floor, his scurried away on all fours with a squeal, as if I didn't exist. Dan looked at me incredulous. "Are you serious? That's it?" A rush of emotions made my chest heave in something that seemed impossible and inevitable at the same time; my face pulled down on itself by sadness. Dan opened his arms and pulled me in close against his warm, wide chest. "It's okay, Mamma, you've done a great job with our boychiks. They're growing up," he said. I was dumbfounded. An era had come to an end and there was nothing I could do about it.

My breasts were returned to me before I was ready to have them back, but life went on. No longer a source of nourishment, they remained larger and more subtle than before I had children. A couple of years after Benya had decided it was time I should close up shop, a friend told me something about breasts I did not fully understand at the time. My boys were still young and my experience from years of nursing still lingered fresh in my body-memory. Yonat was from Israel and a professional puppeteer and the mother of two teenage sons. She was about ten to twelve years older than me, and we met at University of Connecticut in 1988, in a course on the Holocaust. Now, many years later, I was taking her to the airport after one of her visits to the States. We sat down for coffee in the departures area for our final goodbyes, sharing more joys and woes of mothering, couplehood, and life.

"My breasts have given me much more sexual pleasure, the older I've gotten," she said in that direct way Israelis tend to speak. "So, you can look forward to that."

Maybe I had shared with her something intimate about how Dan and I were (or were not) doing at the time. Her words stuck, probably because it was nothing I had ever heard a woman say before, and certainly not to me. What she said also sparked a curiosity in me, an anticipatory levity that I carried with me for several years before one day it hit me. Yonat was right! My breasts were indeed becoming a more relevant and real source for the release of that feel-good hormone oxytocin.

I got to see Yonat once more before I learned the shocking news that she had died of brain cancer. This time I was in Tel Aviv, and we met at a museum exhibit. Over lunch I told her how much her words had stayed with me and how her "breast-pleasure promise" was finally materializing. By then I was in my late forties, divorced, and had a new partner with whom I had discovered new ways of intimacy and eroticism. And it very much involved my breasts both giving and receiving pleasure.

As a younger woman, I had not perceived my breasts as an erogenous zone whose ability and purpose could be to arouse and turn *me* on; I liked the appearance of my then B-cup breasts with their pale pink areolas and understood that they, like breasts in general, played a role in inter-human sexual relations. I enjoyed how my breasts seemed to please lovers, but I did not notice what they felt like, or that there was any the kind of deliciousness generated for *my* benefit when they were fondled, kissed, licked, massaged.

It makes me smile to think that although I shared many intellectual experiences with Yonat during our UCONN days as we'd study for exams and write papers on Hannah Arendt and the Eichmann trial, it's in the breast story that this girl-friend remains the most alive and influential to my life as a woman.

.

Breasts as conduit of nourishment, breasts as providers of pleasure, breasts as victims, breasts as witness.

I'm forty-one years old and I'm standing on the platform of the diving board ten meters up in the air at the outdoor public pool in Oslo. Not a cloud in the sky—a bright, blue expanse above the happy sounds of children and adults as they swim laps, frolic, and slide below. Adrenaline fizzes in my limbs and my heart thumps in my ears as I squirm toward the edge. Lined along the stone border of the round, deep pool, my three middle-school-aged sons cheer me on. The lifeguard, a tanned, blond, young woman in white shorts and tee-shirt with a red cross on its back, gives jumpers the signal by pressing a megaphone to her lips and calling out, "Stand back on the five and seven, go ahead on ten!" That's me, the "ten."

I am about to launch myself freestyle from ten meters up. I will my toes to the tip of the board, and I try not to notice how far away the thirty-three feet to the surface below looks from here; this is what my best friend, Anne—wild, lovable Anne, also a mother of three—has just convinced me to do: "Jump!"

I hear Anne and my boys call out.

"Come on, Mamma! You can do it!"

There is no way out now. The whole park is a movie on pause. I am out of my body and somewhere else. In a flash, I am back to my childhood, when life depended on being cool enough to jump.

But I am not a teenager anymore, I am forty-one and *this is ridiculous*, I hear myself thinking. *I don't have to prove anything to anybody!* I consider that I can and should turn around and climb back down the gleaming and narrow concrete steps, to safety on the ground.

"Go ahead on ten!" the lifeguard repeats loudly, her voice jarring me back to reality. The boys cheer again. Anne whistles loudly.

Ending the torture, I leap. After the initial flapping of my arms, I instinctively slap them tight alongside my thighs, in order to keep my body vertical for impact. *Don't flap your arms! Straight as a nail!* My brain repeats. *Splash!* Then the muffled sound of water all around me as I sink, sink, sink to the depth of the pool, followed by the exhilarating feeling as I reach the water's surface and gasp. *I did it!*

But the full-bodied frame of a woman who has nursed three babies impacts the water differently than that of the lanky teenager I was back in the 1970s. Once out of the pool, my kids flock around me, patting my back and hugging my waist, while I try to ignore that my breasts ache as if they have been beaten by a long wooden board. The boys think I am the coolest mamma around, and Anne—God bless her playfulness—tries to coax me into doing it one more time. "It's always better the second time!" she cajoles. I deflect by offering the kids ice cream.

The next day I discover a red and sore lump, warm and hard on the side of my right breast. I feel feverish. And so, I find myself at the doctor's office telling the funny story while the sixty-something physician feels around for what I guess is an inflammation. And, sure enough, he announces a case of acute mastitis and prescribes a course of antibiotics with hot compresses.

Today, it's my breasts that urge me onward to remember and witness the behavior of the older, white, privileged male physician toward his younger, female patient. Just the doctor and I were in his office, and the door was closed. He was seated at his wooden desk in a Scandinavian and ergonomic office chair, framed photos lining all the surfaces behind him: The Doctor running across a finish line at a marathon, the Doctor riding a horse on a tropical beach, the Doctor on a sailboat, salty and windswept, and the Doctor and his family skiing. It's my breasts that take me back to the room, as if it's happening in real time.

While I sit bare-chested in a chair at the short end of his desk, he rolls his chair over to perform his exam by palpating my breasts. The thing is, he doesn't pull his hands away once he has identified the inflamed lump. Instead, his hands remain there on me, warm, confident, each one gently cupping a breast while lifting them from below, the way a push up bra works.

I don't recall the way his eyes look, only that he looks straight at me and says, "Well, I must say you do have particularly well-formed breasts …"

A flush of heat spreads in my face. *Are you kidding me?* I am embarrassed to admit it, but I think I just smile and say, "well, thank you," as if his words and actions are a gentleman-y thing. It isn't right all along, but I neither do nor say anything else. I sit humiliated, confused, and bare breasted, hearing the words I can't believe I am hearing. I cower yet remain stoic (the part of my Nordic DNA I've had to work hard to de-program, for my emotional and mental health well-being).

I was married mother of three, a confident and independent woman with a PhD, who, as far as I know, did not come across as submissive or vulnerable. Of course, none of this matters in the dynamics of sexual harassment, just like it mattered not to him whether I was weak or strong; to him I was fair game, just like all the other women he had most likely made inappropriate comments to and advances toward in his long, illustrious career as a family doctor.

Looking back, I feel shame and self-criticism that I did not say: "Excuse me, but do you think this is acceptable? Are you out of your fucking mind? Who do you think you are?" Anything would have been better than what I said and didn't do. I was not an insecure teenager, not like I had been when the male gynecologist caressed my butt after I hopped down from the exam table after my first ever OBGYN visit, back in Norway in 1982 when I was seventeen. I should have spoken up then, and I should have in 2006. At least I wish I had. Shrugging it off as gross, male conduct, I have imagined both doctors have since happily retired, with zero bad conscience about their boorish behavior. I admit to lately wishing that they have had to face their accusers and deal with the consequences of their unwanted touching. *I have wished …*

If my breasts had not been involved with such a splash when they hit the surface, I might not remember so clearly that day when I jumped from the thirty-three-foot diving tower. Despite the delightful sounds of my sons' joy and giddiness cheering and whistling me on in cahoots with my best friend Anne, it's my breasts that have played the role of Proust's *Madeleine.* I remember it all so clearly because of *them.*

Nose

To each other, we were as normal and nice
as the smell of bread.
We were just a family. In a family
even exaggerations make perfect sense.
John Irving, *Hotel New Hampshire*

Bacon and eggs sizzling late morning; poached cod or mussels steaming in wine and garlic in the evening—I loved the smells seeping up from the small galley kitchens of the different boats in our Norwegian summers flotilla. In the 1970s, my family spent the several-weeks-long vacation that my parents enjoyed onboard our old, wooden hybrid between a sailboat and a fishing boat. (Ah, Scandinavia, where work-life balance is up front and center in family politics and culture!) Our boat's name, Nabjara, "the round-bellied one" in Hungarian, I was told, was built in Hungary and used for fishing before she was refurbished and sold as a cruiser to a Norwegian, who sold it to my parents. Knowing my father and his propensity for bartering, and for questionable, shady deals, it's quite possible it was a fishy transaction.

The salty, briny smells of seafood bring me back onboard, back on the water. My parents and sister and I lived a lazy, bohemian life, slowly sailing down the southern coast of Norway in the Gulf Stream's gift of often-glorious summer weather, despite our country's northern latitude. My parents' boating friends were our company—up to twenty vessels of varying styles, shapes, and sizes tied up together at sunset in enchanting coves and inlets—a grand flotilla of buoyant, alcohol-infused, loud parties. My sister and I climbed from boat to boat to visit and enjoy the treats offered us by increasingly intoxicated and seemingly happy grown-ups.

One highlight of the summers at sea was wading with my dad into shallow, glimmering, salty water, our bare feet balancing on slippery seaweed and rocks sharp with barnacles, pulling up clusters of salty mussels by the handfuls for steaming on deck.

"We only eat the ones that open up by themselves," my dad warned, "if they stay closed, it means they're no good."

He showed me how to clean the mussels with a knife before putting them into a big pot, and by the time we finished scrubbing the shells, the skin on our hands was shriveled and smelled of brine and seaweed. A mussel feast followed some ten minutes later, when the steam from the pot, infused with a mix of garlic, thyme, and white wine, made my parents' friends rouse from their groggy hangovers and congregate on our expansive and welcoming deck with cigarettes, beers, and wine. The pale and sometimes bright-orange flesh of the mussels tasted salty and sprung spongy against my palate, and every so often I'd bite into a tiny, white pearl that I'd carefully spit out into my hand and save in a small wooden treasure box I kept under the pillow in my bunk.

The summers on the boat were full of other smells I still recognize and can easily evoke, including the warm and oily odor of Nabjara's engine room, where the low, round toilet was rigged on top of planks along one wall, and where we had to balance carefully when the boat was underway, to avoid contact with the engine's scalding metal pipes. Not exactly safe for children, or adults for that matter, which is why we also had a pee-bucket on deck, hidden behind the wheelhouse.

The large main cabin below deck that held our bunks was separated from the engine room by a thin door secured with a small but solid nautical-style brass hook. On most of our parents' friends' boats, the adults had to bend their heads to fit down below, so it was something of a marvel that our entire below deck was fit for a sizable gathering of grown-ups who could all stand up, if they wanted to.

"That cabin is so big you can have a dance party down there!" my mother liked to exclaim.

My sister and I had our own single berths, each attached to the wall a couple of feet up from the floor planks on either side of the ship's hull. We used the wooden bench-seats below our bunks as stepping stools to reach the ladders that took us the rest of the way to our narrow sleeping quarters. A white table edged by a one-centimeter-tall wooden rim, and long, foldable side flaps sat in the middle of the cabin, attached on one side to the base of the massive, round, solid wood mast that ran from the bottom of the hull, fastened below the floor planks, and all the way through the cabin ceiling and on up to above deck, reaching some seven meters/twenty-two feet into the air. On rainy days, we'd eat our meals around this table, the flaps raised to make a nice, big, square surface, the wooden rim preventing items from sliding off during rough seas.

Our parents' berth was wider, although not a full double, and sat lower on the wall, not requiring them to climb up, only to roll into bed. Our bedding had a special smell, a mixture of salty ocean and mold, and most of the time it was a bit damp. On warm, sunny days we'd drag the blankets above deck and hang them on the boom—the smaller horizontal beam perpendicular to the main mast—to air out and dry. But there was nothing I loved more than to curl up in my bunk, moldy or not, surrounded by this summery, musty smell, and fall asleep to the gentle undulations of our boat, the sound of water lapping against the hull, and the sail lines of our and other boats clapping rhythmically against the masts. The distant babble of grownups talking, laughing, and often singing or playing a guitar above deck was familiar and comforting. Even the acrid smell of their cigarette smoke, permeating everything most of the time, became a comfort, because it was familiar. I don't recall it ever bothering me as a child. Sometimes, the grown-ups sat on our boat; other times they'd congregate on the one next to ours, or another one further down the row of the flotilla, but my sister and I always knew our parents were nearby, and we felt safe.

The summer nights were usually mild and always light until past midnight, and the skies were only completely dark for a couple of hours before the sun rose, around 3:30 a.m. I'd wake in the middle of the night to pee, and I'd still hear my parents and their friends partying on. The early mornings were usually quiet as the grownups slept in; perhaps the annual summer radio program "The 9am Hour" sounded at a low volume from someone's cabin. Crawling up on deck, it was bright and warm outside, and through the silence, I'd hear the ocean's gentle movement. The sun glimmered on the water's surface, creating dancing stars that promised another day full of discoveries and freedom from school and schedules. My sister, the other kids, and I would follow our noses and congregate on board the one boat where bacon was simmering in someone's galley, and a lone grownup was willing to put out some breakfast for us. Today, the whiff of propane, that faint rotten-egg-smell, transports me back in time to the memory of the tiny galleys and tasty mealtimes on the water.

All of these are olfactory imprints of my happiest childhood days and my belonging: to the ocean, to a maritime life, to foods from the deep, to family, to discovery, to independence and adventure. I still daydream about life on the water and fantasize about affording a boat one day, and I wonder if I will ever have the opportunity again to feel that same joyful levity of northern summer days as my body tells me I once did. And then I sigh and remember more, and whisper kindly to myself: *of course, you will, Nina.*

Days were spent with the flotilla either sailing to the next stop, or, if we were moored in an exceptionally beautiful and peaceful cove and the weather was nice, we'd stay anchored for a few days in our own little paradise. Nearby, a small island or big rock would beckon the curiosity of us kids, and we'd don our orange life-vests and set out in dinghies on expeditions to explore the unknown land and look for treasures. We felt free and wild; as if we were a gang of happy orphans, we'd climb around the tiny island collecting sticks, stones, seashells, and the occasional bird egg. Sometimes we'd build forts and try to start a fire, and when we got tired or hungry, we'd row ourselves back to the fleet. If days were rainy or cold, we'd spend them below deck, playing cards and board games to candlelight or gas lanterns, listening to the radio, and reading comics.

Sometimes, if some of the adults had rowed out in a dinghy to cast a net at night to be retrieved the next day, and they returned with a jackpot of enough fish for everyone—the favorite being big, healthy cod that swam the Norwegian Sea—we would have a group feast. It was usually my dad or his buddy Bjarne who cleaned the cod on deck under running salt water, then sliced the fish-gut open with deft hands. They prepared hearty steaks for poaching, pulling out innards to show us kids what could be found in the belly of the big fish. Small, limp, translucent crabs and pale remnants of mollusk shells slipped out together with the occasional tiny, half-digested fish, and we squirmed with our "ews" and "cool!" as the salty, ripe sea-smell mixed with the sweet aroma of fresh blood seeped into our nostrils. We moaned as the content of the gooey, slimy guts slid out on the cutting board, combined with stinky fish poop from its intestines.

After the fish were cleaned, somebody would bring up a huge stockpot and the fish would be poached right on deck, while one of us kids would earn a few kroners hosing the fish innards and discarded fins and skin into the sea, through the crack between the deck and the guardrail. Seagulls hovered above, squawking to stake out their territory until they swooshed down with great precision to enjoy the very things we rejected, before they slowly sank into the deep, a feast from above for the scavengers below. The fishy smell lingered on our hands for days. Whenever I clean fish as an adult, I'm transported to these summers on the water and commune, again, with the people, places and moments that filled my childhood world.

.

Mom says, "When we'd come to pick you and your sister up at the end of your farm stay, you reeked to high heaven like the pigsty. As soon as we'd get back home, we'd put you right into a hot bubble bath to soak and run all your clothes in the wash."

Of course, I didn't notice that I stunk like a working farm.

The remaining weeks of school vacation not spent on our boat were spent in the calm of the inland countryside, far from the familiar smells of ocean air, seafood, and seaweed. Urban working parents like mine paid farm families to keep us city kids housed, fed, and mostly happy, involved with farm animals in bucolic surroundings several hours away from our home in the bustling Oslo capital.

Whenever I drive by farm fields in my adult life in New England, I roll down the windows and breathe in deeply the smell of manure, which makes me smile despite its distinct sulfide and ammonia stench. The rank odor of chicken-shit fertilizer and working farm life—grain, mud, feed, and cut grass—takes me back to all the summers I spent as a child in the Norwegian countryside. Though I was usually happy as a pig in shit, it was also a time of homesickness and lessons in survival.

Life on the farm with the other city kids, around fifteen to twenty of us in total, was at times quite Orwellian. I quickly learned to fend for myself against merciless, bigger kids, and, later, when my sister, six years younger, joined me at "summer colony," as it was called, I had to protect both of us. As soon as the farmer and his wife were out of sight, there was plenty of teasing and kids teaming up against each other. Was I an unkind kid, too, or a victim? Most likely, I was a bit of both; taking shit and throwing it back just as hard.

Once, I was climbing a ladder leaning up against the outside back wall of the boys' bathroom to sneak a peek at them through the small window left ajar, when I was suddenly discovered by one of them. With a vicious smile, he pushed the window outward, causing me to fall into the lush, tall patch of burning nettle below. In stinging agony, I later sat on a low kitchen stool in the middle of the barnyard, whimpering, wearing only my underpants and a sleeveless t-shirt, while one of the adults smeared cool, pasty, pink calamine lotion all over my blotchy, burning body, as the other kids—especially the boys—leered and made fun. The sweet, chalky smell of the calamine lingers as a memory not of pain as much as of humiliation.

The feeling was triumphant when, to boost my morale after the burning nettle incident, farmer Olsen let me ride with him in the cabin of the huge tractor he took to the fields, or, even more exciting, let me sit on the back of the *skurtresker*, the combine harvester, when he cut the fields. In that moment I was the boss-girl. I owned the farm. I was on top of the farm-life hierarchy (this was also a moment when the gentle stirrings of my first and innocent childhood crush tickled my insides: Olsen was a handsome man in his thirties, and though I would never have recognized it as such at the time, reflecting on it now, that part fondness part fascination—that unarticulated desire to be closer, be the chosen one—makes me smile in recognition.

Getting to ride on the harvester meant clutching onto a small, metal ledge with your feet dangling behind the massive machine, and with strict instructions that if you fell off, to walk straight back to the farm rather than to run after the loud harvester and all its rotating, sharp blades. Farmer Olsen couldn't hear anything due to the blast of the engine and his ear protectors, so there would be no use trying to call for help.

The smell of the newly cut hay was raw and golden the way it haloed around me, as dust and pieces of straw stuck to my clothing, hair, ears, and face, filling and tickling my nostrils.

Old letters home, saved by my mom and glued into family photo albums, reveal in clumsy handwriting that I had fun and loved the animals, but that I was also homesick and reported having peed in bed. The last line of one letter from the early 1970s reads, "So, therefore I want you to come and pick me up this weekend." This my parents did not do; I was there for the long haul, usually three to four weeks.

When pick-up day finally came, the farmer's mutt barked at all the commotion of kids reuniting with their parents. Seeing my parents pull into the barnyard was a great moment. I'd run to the pigpen to show them how big the piglets had gotten during my stay. I'd point out my favorite one—the tiniest one that looked like it needed extra love and protection—and demonstrate how to hold it just right, one hand under its belly and one draped over its back to keep it safe from falling, just like farmer Olsen had shown us. Then it was on to the barn to introduce them to my favorite horse, Stella, whom I'd ridden bareback in the fields all summer, holding onto the mane and clutching my legs around her round, warm belly.

Despite getting carsick on the curvy country roads home, I'd fill their ears with stories about how farmer Olsen used big, metal pliers to pull the baby teeth from the piglets so they wouldn't bite their mothers' teats, and what it sounded like when they squealed, and how we got to hold their pink and clean little compact bodies and comfort them once the dentistry was done. I can still hear the snap of the teeth breaking off at their bases, and the squeaks of piglets with their little wet, wiggly snouts and their fluttering towhead eyelashes. I'd hold the piglet tight and lift it toward my face and let my lips rest on its warm skin while inhaling an aroma of sawdust and the warm, sweet-smelling flesh of the still-clean babes. The knowledge that this cute little helpless thing would soon turn into one of the huge, filthy, stinky hogs out in the muddy pen, and then eventually to bacon, was enough to make me cry. I wanted to take the piglets home.

.

Connecticut Route 44 runs along farms, fields and modest homes, and represents the longest stretch that connects the highway from the urban center of Hartford, where I lived for thirty years, to the rural setting of the University of Connecticut's Storrs campus, where I attended classes as a commuting student through my bachelor's (French and Jewish Studies), master's, and PhD degrees (French). Farm stands, "antique" dealers and the occasional ice cream stand sit along the two-lane road with a double-yellow line between lanes, and the occasional stop sign or light.

On my many years of long commutes to campus, the whiffs of cow manure and chicken shit scattered on the fields as fertilizer along Route 44 brought me right back to my childhood summers at the Olsen's farm, and also evoked happy days at the urban stable in Oslo, where I mucked stalls, groomed horses, and rode mares, geldings, and the occasional stallion throughout my teenage years. Passing those rural Connecticut fields, rain or shine, I'd roll down the window of my car and take several deep inhales, grinning dreamily, transported to a good place as if I were an addict who'd just gotten her fix of something that could transport her to somewhere glorious and far away. The horse manure in Oslo smelled better and less like methane than the Connecticut fields, and I used to love gripping the wooden handle of the pitchfork with its four long, strong, metal teeth, while sifting through the horses' sawdust bedding to separate out the clusters of tennis-ball-sized dung. Some still warm, they were speckled with remnants of tiny golden husks from the grains in their feed.

In the depth of Oslo winters, the piles of poop steamed when I'd wheel them out back to the muck shed, where in the bin next door, I'd fill the wheelbarrow with clean, fine, wood shavings mixed with sawdust from fragrant cedar and pine, to refresh the stalls. The familiar wooden scents evoke the same visceral nostalgia as the chicken and cow shit in the fields. The chores at the stable gave me a sense of competency from a young age, and I would quickly notice that the stable manager, a middle aged, grey-haired and jovial man from Denmark named Ingemann, appreciated my contributions in the mucking department. He smiled and called out my name, and liked to joke around, making me feel grownup and part of the extended stable family.

Ingemann's assistant, Jon, was a younger and slightly daft but friendly fellow. Grinning, he wore suspenders pulled taut over his round belly, and always tall, hunter green, rubber boots. When it was time to feed the horses, the dozen or so young kids like me who hung around the stable would line up, and as Ingemann or Jon handed us buckets filled with just the right kind of feed mix for each horse, they'd call out the names of each one awaiting their meal. "Max!" "Diankas!" "Silver!" The buckets heavy in our hands, the sweet and thick aroma of moist molasses clumps mixed with the dry grains followed us as our job was to find the right horse as fast as we could (and the veterans among us knew exactly where each stall was located in the expansive stable that housed over fifty horses), open the stall door, dump the feed into the trough without spilling, and run back to have the bucket filled anew for the next hungry steed. It took a certain amount of confidence to do the feeding because the horses would always get excited hearing and smelling the daily feeding under way, and were often moody and feisty, neighing and snorting, stomping and pacing, as they anticipated their chow. Not all the kids who took riding lessons dared to take active part of this ritual because of the heightened energy of the feeding frenzy, but it was a satisfying routine for us regulars.

Hay, horse shit, molasses, grain, the distinct smell of hooves being cleaned and cut, the saltlick attached on the wall in each horse's bin, and the musky, almost peppery odor from the horse's sweaty hair when I removed the saddle and saddle pad after a ride: all odors my nose recognizes from my formative teenage years at the stables.

As a kid, I'd often stick my nose into places where it didn't necessarily belong, like when I'm twelve and babysitting two-year-old Nora, the only child of our upstairs neighbors Brita and Tore. In 1977, we live on the first floor, and they live on the fourth and top floor of our brick apartment complex in Oslo, built in 1929. Above Brita and Tore's apartment and all the top-floor apartments, is a huge, shared attic, only reachable from our kitchen doors leading to the common back staircase, which is wooden, narrow, and steep. Once I get to the attic from the back stairs, I can walk the entire block from building to building by going from attic to attic separated only by a door that stays closed but not locked for fire safety.

I love the way the attic smells: dry, dusty, and like the old wooden furniture and belongings that tenants and owners store there. Occasionally, I hear the flutter of pigeons' wings, as they come in for shelter through the rooftop-hatches left open by our janitor, Mr. Isachsen, to air out the attic. In each attic space, there is a storage bin for every apartment unit in that building. All the buildings on our red-bricked block were built the same year and are connected, and together form a perfect square block with a shared inner courtyard.

Even though we are just supposed to keep stuff in our own attic storage bins divided by chain link fence walls, some people have larger pieces of furniture to store that won't fit inside their bins. These sit along the tall walls under dark gabled attic ceilings; ignored, extinct creatures waiting to be brought back to life and made relevant again in the company of the families and homes where they belong.

Brita and Tore have a massive armoire stored in the attic, and it isn't locked. On one of my expeditions, I open the doors with the tiny antique key that sits in the lock as if waiting for me to turn it, an invitation, really, and the heavy doors swing open with a creak. Stuffed inside I discover bags stacked upon bags with clean, neatly folded tiny baby clothes that Nora must have outgrown. They smell like roses and are so cute I can't resist unfolding some to look at them. Then I remember the real-size baby-doll named Anita that I have in my room, and I imagine how perfect these baby clothes will look on her instead of the fake, store-bought doll clothes I have. I pack up a bag and tell myself I am just going to borrow them for a little while.

Did I return them to the armoire? I hope I did. I know I had to hide the clothes from my mother because she would have become suspicious if she saw Anita the doll dressed up in clothes she had never seen before, and that were obviously real baby clothes. I wanted to show my mom and grand-mother how cute my doll looked, but had to hide the loot and my thievery, which took away some of the pleasure of dressing up my doll. Nobody to share it with.

Being snoopy brought a certain loneliness, although I wonder now if perhaps the loneliness preceded being snoopy? Between my two often-absent working parents and the laid-back parenting culture of 1970s Scandinavia, I was left to my own devices from an early age, never overprotected or ques-tioned too much about my whereabouts.

As a youngster, I'm deeply intrigued by the couple of Brita and Tore because they are so unlike my own parents. Brita has black hair and olive skin, and a flat, dark, birthmark the shape of an island takes up part of her right cheek. She often wears a long, black mink coat, even over her pajamas, and smokes her cigarettes with an elegant, black cigarette holder accented by a golden ring. She smokes all the time and everywhere, walking around enveloped in an enigmatic cloud.

Tore isn't too tall and has a mustache and I think he's hand-some even though he is balding. When he leaves our building, his Paco Rabanne cologne lingers heavy in the stairwell, and I'm excited to think that I may run into him when the smell seems especially fresh. Sometimes I open the door to our apartment just to stick my head out to catch a whiff of his almost presence. I watch my early tween crush hop into (what I recall as) his forest green, vintage convertible sportscar from behind my parents' bedroom curtains.

When I look after baby Nora and she is sleeping, I rummage their apartment. Eternally inquisitive, I am often told to stop sticking my nose into everything, especially by my grand-mother *Besta*, my father's mother, who always keeps a close eye on me when I spend time with her; she must have noticed her granddaughter's snooping. But my curiosity is a gateway to interesting discoveries and poking around is my specialty. I have no idea what I am looking for in Brita and Tore's apartment, but I open every drawer, closet, armoire, and chest, lifting and sifting and peeking, smelling and squeezing and turning objects in my hands to discover more layers, maybe even secrets.

Brita's make-up table is especially fascinating, a whole landscape of sensuous discoveries. Lipsticks and mascaras in fancy gold cases, colorful eyeshadows and powders and creams that smell flowery. Even though she smokes incessantly, her clothes smell good, and she has fancy cashmere sweaters in pink, cream, and black. She wears pearl and diamond earrings and keeps her jewelry in small, delicate porcelain dishes in their bedroom, which is dark and stuffed with closets and clothes. It's exciting and naughty and I love to run my fingers over their stuff that smells different than the things we have at home. An entire universe of *difference and discovery* offering itself up to the greedy, probing, hungry seeker that was me as a kid, lodging itself deep in my memory as an olfactory gift to be recovered and marveled at, some forty-plus-years later.

.

Today, I look at my nose with its imperfections, a small mole here, some broken capillaries there, and still appreciate it for working well, for keeping me, mostly, out of trouble. I've smelled fire when the gas was once accidentally left open on our range and gotten the whiff of an electrical short spewing tiny sparks and smoke, the potential for a real, deadly fire.

How often does my nose *not* recognize when something smells fishy, like forgotten leftovers deep in the bowels of our fridge, that I might have otherwise eaten (the green, furry stuff on top might also be a sign)? Once, I did not heed the "something smells fishy" warning of my acute nose at a kosher restaurant in Queens with my then husband and his lovable brood of New York cousins. When the Moroccan lamb dish I had ordered with glee (lamb, my all-time favorite meat, despite my more recent vegetarian ambitions) was placed before me, I noticed a whiff of what I thought might be the odor of meat gone bad. Mildly sour, fetid, with hints of sulfur, it lingered heavy but briefly in my nose. However, I did not want to make everyone wait more than we already had for service and figured (or hoped) maybe it was just my imagination because it wasn't *that* bad and tasted okay what with all the exotic cumin, cinnamon, and turmeric. So, I ate it anyway. In the car on the way home to Connecticut on I-95, just as we passed Co-Op City in the Bronx, the wrath of my insulted intestines unleashed itself. My nose tried but failed to protect me, and it was a memorable day I'd like to forget.

Skin

Ce qu'il y a de plus profond dans l'homme, c'est sa peau.
The deepest part of a human being is her/his skin.
Paul Valéry

When I wake up the morning after our first day of glorious cross-country skiing, I can tell immediately that something is wrong with my skin. It is difficult to open my eyes, and as I stumble out of bed and face the tiny mirror hanging crooked on the round-timbered cabin wall, I gasp at my reflection. I'm thirteen years old and on skiing vacation in the mountains of Norway with my girlfriend Anette, her mom Martha and her mom's new boyfriend, the handsome Rolf. The small bedroom in this modest Norwegian mountain-cabin spins around me. I look at myself again in the spotted mirror and I lean closer toward the shape staring back at me, but it's a face I can't recognize.

My skin is so sunburned that my forehead is protruding, swollen above my blond eyebrows. A rush of adrenaline shoots through me. I try to make sense of what's going on. I want to blink but everything is puffy and thick and sore. I tell myself I'm probably dreaming; if I go back to sleep it will all go away, and I can wake up looking normal. But every time

I look up at my forehead—I can't stop myself from checking again and again the grotesque deformity that is my face—the whole area above my brow crinkles hard and seems about to crack open along the creases in the burnt skin. When I reach up and touch my forehead, I press down with my finger and it feels squishy, as if I'm checking rising dough.

Anette is still asleep in the top bunk, her breath slow and regular. I hear the grownups making breakfast in the room next door. There are giggles and hushed voices.

I wish it were my mom and dad out here. I don't want Anette to wake up since I'm sure she will freak out when she sees me. She might even scream. But Anette inevitably stirs now. The bright morning sun glimmers through the small square windowpanes and the smells from the kitchen begin to awaken her. I quietly slip back into my bottom bunk and pull the covers over my head; I don't want to see anyone and, most of all, I don't want anyone to see me.

There's a knock and I hear the door open.

"Good morning, girls! Breakfast is ready in five minutes!" Rolf's cheery voice rings out.

I don't answer from under my covers, feigning sleep, but Anette mumbles from her bed as she stretches.

"What time is it? Is the sun shining?"

"The sun is out and we've got another perfect day of skiing ahead of us!" Rolf answers, upbeat.

"Mmmmmm, I'm still tired," Anette moans and stretches again above me.

"It's nine o'clock and time to hop to it! Too much fun and card-playing last night," he adds with a chuckle.

We like Rolf a lot because he is both younger and more fun than Martha's strict ex-boyfriend, Jack. He had grey hair around a balding head and walked in a stiff way, tilting to one side, and we never knew if he'd be in a bad or good mood. Jack would stick his head through the door and tell us to stay in Anette's tiny room to play quietly or to go outside, even though his apartment was huger than any I had ever seen. And he never smiled, never laughed. He drove a fancy white Jaguar with red leather seats, soft and cool against our thighs, and on a rare occasion we'd get to ride in it, which I thought was the coolest thing ever. *So fancy!*

I am still quiet under the covers, but it's getting warm in here. My face is not only stiff and crinkly but also fiery hot.

"Anette?" I say peeking out, the cool air in our unheated bedroom soothing my skin.

"Good morning, Nina!" she chirps, greeting me and the day full of energy and joy. "Slept good down there?"

"Something is wrong with my face," I begin.

"What do you mean, wrong?"

"It's all swollen and I look … funny," I say.

She is quiet for a few seconds and then her face drops down from the side of the top bunk; she looks at me upside down, her pageboy haircut dangling. Anette has bright, blue eyes surrounded by dark, full eyelashes, and most of the boys at school and in our neighborhood have a crush on her. Her mom and dad were famous models when they were in their twenties, her dad a prize-winning athlete who held the national record in sprint. But then he died of cancer when Anette was a baby, and at school we all felt sorry for her.

"Wow!" She is staring at me as if trying to find the me that she knows. Then she starts to laugh.

"Sorry, I don't mean to laugh! But you look so weird!"

"I know," I say, "it hurts."

I know she isn't laughing to be mean, but her reaction makes the lump in my stomach heavier, and a wave of homesickness washes over me. Tears well in my almost-swollen-shut eyes, and when I try to wipe the tears away, it hurts even more.

"What happened to you?"

"I don't know," I say as I turn toward the wall, away from her gaze.

I know whatever is wrong with me must be some kind of accident, but I don't want to show the grown-ups either because their reactions will make me feel even worse. And what if all this will ruin our vacation and I'll have to go home? I have looked so much forward to being here with my friend, and since my family doesn't own a cabin, it's super special to be here.

The two-bedroom cabin is small and cozy, simply furnished with plain pine beds, tables, and chairs; pillows and cushions covered by wool fabric in traditional Norwegian mountain-cabin colors—muted blue, red or greens—propped in the corners of the sectional couch. An antique painted shelf, with a strip of embroidered and pressed white cotton border attached to the front, adorns the wall above the table. It displays a mix of vintage plates with different designs held in place behind a round, wooden bar. The living room has a kitchenette in one corner, and through the small-paned double window above the counter, a snow-covered mountain range stretches bluish and grand, far off in the horizon.

Lying in bed, I think about Anette's mom, who happens to be a beautician; skin is her specialty! Maybe she will be able to help me, rescue me even. But I'm afraid to step out of bed and into the daylight because hiding my face and myself in bed allows me to avoid facing my awful reality, even if just temporarily.

The morning sun hits the snowy peaks and makes for a magical display of light and shapes; sights like these inspired the painters whose art is found in our national fairytales. Since there is no running water or electricity, we must carry buckets from a brook a few meters behind the cabin, and we use a propane cooking stovetop and lots of candles for light in the evenings. The outhouse, located just a few steps from the front door, has a small heart carved into the middle of the door, and the seat inside is wooden, which makes it comfortable to sit on, even in the bitter cold. There's a shovel and a broom leaning against the outhouse wall and a big, fat nail to hang the flashlight on at night, pokes out from the wooden trim of the door.

We don't think about everything Rolf's cabin doesn't have, such as water, electricity, or indoor plumbing because there is plenty of wood for the fireplace and we play Crazy Eight and Yahtzee by candlelight in the evenings, enjoy easy meals like traditional sour cream porridge, slathered with melted butter, sugar, and cinnamon and accompanied by salted, dried, and cured lamb shanks. Because it is Easter, Anette and I each have our own big, papier-mâché Easter egg decorated with a pastel-colored print depicting chicks, flowers and bunnies, and the eggs are filled heavy with our favorite chocolates and candies. We carefully parcel out the contents to make it last as long as possible, since we are here for five days and there will be no shopping or chances for refills once the eggs are empty.

The day before, while we were all out on the trails, Martha and Rolf must have been happy when Anette and I suggested they head back to the cabin so that we—mature young women that we thought we were—could continue to explore the groomed trails by ourselves. Expansive and powdery plateaus beckoned us with mystical, wintery shimmers in the full, midday sun. That was all well and fine except we never realized that the sunscreen had gone back to camp with the amorous adults. We had all the other critical things in our pouches: two oranges, two Norwegian equivalents of Kit Kat candy bars called *Kvikk Lunsj,* and a thermos filled with hot cocoa. But no sunscreen.

The power of the sun's destructive rays was far from our minds as we were surrounded by breathtaking summits and groomed cross country trails, and, besides, Anette did not have the same fair skin I had. She always got a golden tan, so there was no skin-protective groupthink. We just repeated, "Aren't we lucky to have such great weather during our vacation!"—a common Norwegian mantra when the weather is good—and savored the sensation of enough sunny warmth against our clothing and skin that we could shed our anoraks, and maybe even the wool sweaters underneath. We'd tie the wind and waterproof layers triumphantly around our waists and with great, big sighs, take a seat in the impromptu snow-chairs we built beside the trail with our mitten-clad hands. Basking in such glee, I simply did not think about how exposed my face was at this altitude, and how, for someone fair-skinned like me, this was a very, very bad thing to forget.

Eventually, I have to get out of bed and join everyone for breakfast in the other room. While I dress, I hear Anette tell her mom about me in a hushed voice, and when I open our bedroom door, Martha's eyes meet mine, compassion filling the distance between us.

"Oh, Nina, what has happened with your face?" she says as she approaches me. "Let me take a look." The beautician specializing in skin issues leans in with confidence.

"This is a very bad sunburn, Nina," she says in her soft, sing-songy accent from southern Norway, her hands cool and gentle on my face. "Considering the swelling and the heat, I think it's probably a third-degree one." She looks at me with pity and puts wet face cloths on my forehead to soothe the aggravated skin. She has all sorts of cooling creams that smell flowery and grown-up like her skin-care salon in Oslo, and she gently spreads some on my cheeks, forehead, and around my eyes.

I love the special attention she gives me, and all the pleasant smells from the ointments, but my vacation is ruined. I have to stay inside for the next two days, and I am only able to go back outside on the third day because it is overcast. I don't remember much else from that whole week, but I am sure we play plenty of cards, Monopoly, and pick-up sticks, read books and knit in front of the fire. Eventually the swelling goes down, and my skin peels off in large, translucent and papery flakes with silky and soft, jagged edges; I gently pull off the dead skin flakes to see how big they can get before they separate fully from my face. Underneath the old skin, a new layer appears, rosy pink, delicate, and tender.

Forgetting to put on sunscreen and suffering from a third-degree burn as a result should have been a mistake I'd make only once. But it was not.

.

I sit in the UCONN Dermatology office in Farmington, Connecticut, with a wad of forms to fill out on my lap, neatly arranged on a clipboard. I'm about forty years old, married, with three middle-schoolers. From the TV screen on the far wall in the waiting room, a woman with perfect make-up and hair talks energetically about the benefits of some skin treatment.

Brochures of facial and different types of plastic surgery services are stacked in clear acrylic holders on window ledges and table-tops.

My thick stack of papers takes forever to fill out—so many questions! Entire health histories to be charted, not just mine but my parents' and sibling's as well. I sigh, flip the pages and scan the endless blanks, and return to the first page with resolve to plough through before I'm called in. When I get to the page about my skin history, things get gritty.

"Do you typically get sunburned?"—Yes.

"How would you describe your sunburns? Mild, moderate or severe?"—Mild to very little in the last years, moderate in my twenties, severe a few times in my childhood and teens.

"Have you used tanning beds?"—Yes (Don't ask me why).

"Have you or any of your parents had basal cell or squamous cell cancer, or melanoma? If so which type, where, and at what age?—Yes, father, forehead, about age sixty.

"Do you use sunscreen? Always/Sometimes/Never." —Rarely as a youngster, usually as an adult.

"Is there anything in particular you would like to discuss with the doctor today?"—Yes. I have noticed a couple of moles on my right shin that itch and I'd like them checked out.

The questions on the forms scare me and I am suddenly faced with the clinical reality of the lack of awareness in the 1960s and 70s regarding sun-protection, and also the vanity and stupidity of the adult me. Tanning beds? Really, Nina ... What brought a fair-skinned, easily sunburned Scandinavian woman to pay handsomely to undress and lie between two cold glass surfaces filled with long fluorescent bulbs that emit both UVA and UVB rays, the latter known to cause skin damage and cancer?

It was the 1990s and I was in my twenties not yet a mother, and it was only later, as a parent, that the idea of my own mortality would shift from vague awareness to obsessive fear. Sure, I had read that it was not advisable to use tanning beds, but vanity pushed me to buy a three-month pass during one dismal New England winter season. I was yearning to get rid of my pallor and acquire me some "healthy" glow. Back in Norway, I had also heard that sunlamps were considered good for Vitamin D absorption (or production?) and helpful in controlling the much-dreaded seasonal affective disorder that a large percentage of my Norwegian *landsmen* are known to experience. This type of cyclic depression is also connected with alcoholism and the tragic peak in suicides during the long, dark months. My own cousin Jonas suffered from this disorder and died of an overdose in his twenties. During summers, he was typically happy and would gain weight and be hopeful about life, and drink less, eat more, sleep better, and be more social. Winter months were like a heavy shade that enveloped his soul; his body withered, he withdrew, became depressed, and used alcohol and pills to dull the hopelessness and pain he experienced.

In my twenties, I did not yet think much about the possible genetic links between my own mood swings and occasional depressions, and the depression and suicide of my grandfather, who was my cousin Jonas's grandfather as well. Einar Boug, my mother's father, died of a self-administered morphine overdose three years before I was born. Jovial, popular and athletic (an amateur welterweight boxer and soccer player), he was an MD in private practice but also an insulin-dependent diabetic whose second marriage was crumbling, and personal finances were in dire straits. My mom was twenty-five when she found him slumped over his desk in his home office. He was fifty-two.

At the time of my suntan-bed subscription, I did not think either that there might be dots to connect between my beloved father's later-in-life alcoholism, possibly spurred on by depression (or was it the other way around?), and my own periodic melancholy.

Rather, it seemed as if I was intuitively drawn to the "advantages" of what tanned skin promised. My mother and the women of her generation's use of aluminum-foil-covered trays under their chins while facing the sun combined with all the advertising in the eighties conditioned me during my formative years. Being tanned was a sure way to feel healthy, gorgeous, and desired.

I recently read a Facebook post titled "Twenty Things Women Should Stop Wearing After the Age of Thirty: 1-20: The weight of other people's expectations and judgments." What's not to love about this? However, what are we to do with the weight of the expectations and judgments we impose on ourselves? Deprogramming takes a long, long time, as I have learned. Thankfully, something magic often happens once we reach menopause. It's pay-back time: many of us stop giving a fuck.

In the exam room at UCONN Dermatology, I tell my dermatologist about how I've had several moles removed in my teens while I still lived in Norway, and how I have been sunburned a lot throughout my life. While she flips through the pages about the medical history of my skin, I also tell her that none of the removed moles were cancerous, just "irregular."

"Well, based on the information you are giving me here," she says and looks at me through metal-rimmed bifocals, "if you were my daughter, I would want you to have a baseline digital file done." She is a nationally recognized melanoma and skin cancer expert, has a no-nonsense salt-and-pepper short haircut and stands tall and lean in her white lab coat. She tells me about this most advanced method of surveillance for moles, so that there will be a recorded "before" picture of every single pigment spot on my body, against which she can compare each one as it appears in real time, as years go by. Any change in color, shape, or size will be detectible through the handy-dandy magnifying loupe.

She bends down over my bare shin, holding the loupe closely over the questionable moles I have identified.

"It's not inexpensive and not covered by insurance," she adds without looking up, checking spots on my thighs, calves, and feet. She motions for me to put my foot up on a stool and she separates my toes and checks between each one.

"Not inexpensive, as in?" I ask.

"About $600."

I gulp, but also know that if she says I should, it's the thing to do, so I agree.

"Okay, good," she says. "I'll get Gary my assistant in here—he's the specialist with the digital camera—and then we'll get it done quickly."

Gary, I think. Great. Now a dude is going to be taking close ups of every square centimeter of my naked body.

"You'll have to take off all your clothes, but you can keep the smock on and we'll work our way around; just leave it open in the front." She looks at me, gives a quick, efficient smile with a nod, and then leaves the room before I have time to respond.

I sit on the edge of the exam table and try to come to terms with the fact that I will shortly be standing butt naked in front of this Gary, likely covered in goose bumps, my nipples erect.

Turns out that Gary is a lovely guy; why wouldn't he be? With round, red cheeks and thinning hair, he smiles and tries his best to not look at me in any way that might feel uncomfortable for me—or look as if looking is not what he is doing—and his mannerisms are gentle, his voice, too. He fiddles intently with the computer screen and the digital camera, and when he snaps away from my head to my toes (and in-between the toes, as well as the inside of the thighs, under the breasts that I must lift ceremoniously, one at a time) he makes small-talk and laughs at my jokes, humor being my go-to bolstering mechanism.

When he is done taking all the photos, my dermatologist returns. It's really something else to see an entire big and bright computer screen filled with side-by-side images of one's naked body in all its moley glory. Like a collage or cartoon, frames sit side by side, each revealing a change in positions and angles of the character that is me, my headless body with all its skin, wanting to tell its story.

When I gave birth the third and last time, a momentarily dramatic scene occurred involving the umbilical cord and a clot causing my blood to squirt all over the delivery room walls, ceiling, and midwife's glasses and face (see "Vagina"). After that, I decided nothing bodily could ever embarrass me again. *Bring it on*, I think with a sigh, facing the brutally honest and (photo-)graphic representations of the bright-white skin of mine in the shapes of breasts, hips, butt, thighs, and all the rest of the nooks and crannies, bends and angles of my pale surfaces. Gary scrolls through the images, about twenty in all on the "mole map," as it's called, to make sure he's got the whole of me covered. If I have any suspicious moles in the future, I am in as good hands as it gets; a little safer, I think, and look away.

On the lower part of my belly, between my belly button and the hairline of my *mons pubis*, several now-pale stretchmarks on my skin speak of the physical charge of the three pregnancies I had in rapid succession between the ages of twenty-nine and thirty-three. When I stand naked in front of a full-length mirror, I see these bluish-pinkish and squiggly lines that tell the story of my dramatically stretched skin; with each nine-month gestation, I gained between twenty-five and forty-five pounds. This always sounded strange to me, considering each baby came out weighing "just" about ten pounds. These Viking boychiks arrived more than fully formed and ready to invade—or was it raid?—my world and my body. But what was all that other weight? I've learned that blood-volume increases by about fifty percent each time a woman is pregnant, and this surely accounted for some of it, but the rest remains a blurry mystery of enlarged organs, fluids, evolutionary-related protection of fetus, and, I guess, accumulated fat deposits (added to my hips for said protection of fetus).

In their unison, these raised and dipping impressions on the skin of my belly will forever remind me of a sweeping time in my life, where not only my skin was stretched but my whole person as well. I pushed my mind and body in a search for meaning and happiness, but also, to some extent, in an effort to please. After three years of intense studies with an orthodox rabbi, and enough courses in Jewish Studies at UCONN to earn a degree, I converted to Judaism before Dan and I got married.

When it came to creating my Jewish family, and my newly minted Jewish identity, I have had literal skin in the game. Not only was my Viking DNA a welcome addition to the Eastern European Ashkenazi gene pool of Dan's family, and our children anxiously awaited and welcomed, but emotionally, the commitment to this "new" Jewish life I had chosen was a deeply *physical* and *material* commitment. Judaism is less about faith than action, and it's in the doing that the Jewish traditions and identity are cemented. You can believe with all your heart (and even understand) that circumcising your son is an important part of Jewish identity and continuity, but handing over your eight-day-old newborn to be cut into with a scalpel, in the presence of your community and your incredulous non-Jewish mother, (hailing from a culture that does not circumcise), is a whole different commitment. Not only did I have metaphorical skin in the game, but I put my newborn son's actual skin in it, too.

Tobias is eight days old, and his circumcision, or *brit milah*—the covenant of circumcision—welcomes him into our Jewish community and the entire Jewish tribe. The ceremony and celebration are held in the synagogue where Dan and I belong. Friends, family, and all our extended family fill the sanctuary. There are close to one hundred guests. My mother arrived from Norway eight days ago, on the day I gave birth. She and I stand in the women's section, two rows away from the stage where Rabbi Alter performs the circumcision (our rabbi is also a *mohel*, a Jew trained in the practice of *brit milah*, ritual circumcision). My father-in-law sits on a tall, carved wooden chair with regal, red velvet upholstery, his firstborn grandson nestled on pillow on his lap, a white, silken prayer shawl draped over the patriarch's shoulders and his *yarmulke* perched on his bald, shiny head. My husband stands tall next to his dad, and he sways slowly from side to side, clutching a prayer book, a *siddur*, to his chest. I can tell he is in a deep place, part anxious, part exhilarated. Our rabbi talks briefly to the gathering about how each baby is born with great potential, that we are about to honor the covenant between Abraham and God which has defined the Jewish people for millennia. Despite the rabbi's beaming face and gentle voice, I worry that my mom must think it all sounds crazy, and I look over at her and meet her eyes with a smile, as if to soothe the strangeness she might feel. She does not smile back.

When the rabbi turns and bends over Tobi, the room falls silent. The baby is quiet as well, content and dozing because I have just fed him. But that quickly changes when his romper is unbuttoned and his diaper removed, and the rabbi deftly prepares and snips my son's foreskin. He yelps and begins to whimper, and my mother-in-law, who stands on my other side, takes my hand in hers and squeezes it. She smiles through tears of joy, a Jewish grandson! The baby's crying stops within seconds as the rabbi touches a gauze pad, soaked in the iconic sweet and kosher Manischewitz wine, to my newborn's lips. An age-old custom: let the baby suck enough on the wine-soaked cloth until he settles and falls back asleep.

My mother is ashen as the rabbi chants blessings in Hebrew amidst "*Amens!*" and "*Mazel tovs!*" from those gathered to witness and celebrate the new member of the tribe. Then he loudly announces the name of the new little community member: *Tuvia Yaakov Meir ben Chune Moshe*. My son has a Hebrew name, which will be used in religious contexts, and an English one which honors both his American and Norwegian heritage: Tobias Thor Lichtenstein.

I look at Dan, who stands on the stage of the sanctuary, in front of the ark that holds the Torah scrolls, while our son's chosen godparent carries my baby toward me. But I am cold sweating because I can sense how incredibly foreign and difficult this event is for my mom, while at the same time, I am proud and feel an intense sense of belonging to my new Jewish community. Such mixed emotions: I am dizzy, the moment surreal. My mother grips the back of the seat in front of her while fighting back tears, and I think I hear her mumble, "Barbarians."

.

"When we are sad, and angry, and lost, and lonely, our skin bubbles, and itches, and weeps," notes Christina Patterson, one of the contributing authors in *Beneath the Skin: Great Writers on the Body*. My skin, as it turns out, is no exception. At some point during these early child-rearing years (remember, I had three kids in four years), the skin on my heels was so cracked that I was barely been able to walk, and it was not from being overweight. For a period, my scalp was so irritated I developed crusty scabs from all the scratching. I didn't think about my skin in connection with my emotional life, back then. I was often uncomfortable with how it felt, how it itched and cracked, but I never connected the dots.

Around four years after Tobi's circumcision, the familiarity of my mom's voice from across the Atlantic Ocean reminds me how homesick I am. On this day, I hold the phone between my shoulder and ear, hands busy changing my youngest and third son Benya's diaper. Suddenly I am a daughter, a child even more than a mother. Tears well up from somewhere deep inside while the baby participates in the conversation in his own way, with blabbers and coos. His dimpled hands clutch a small plastic mirror framed in primary colors, his plump four-month-old body propped on a foamy changing pad strapped to the top of the washer in a corner of our messy kitchen.

Home videos from these early years of my boys' lives reveal a clutter all around the house that today strikes me as strange and unfamiliar: Toppling piles of books, toys, and clothing strewn on counters, chairs, and tables, Legos scattered on the floor, bulletin-boards stuffed with layers of drawings, kindergarten certificates and school pictures. The images resuscitate visceral memories of how full this time in my life really was, and how tapped out I was. How stretched I was.

I've called my mom because I am exhausted and wish she were with me in America to help with my three little active boys, our cavernous, impractical old house, and our two dogs always underfoot, eternally seeking the pre-children lovin' in which they basked only four years earlier. The dirty diaper I've folded and set aside slides off the surface and lands on the floor with a thump, heavy from pee and poop. The passing whiff hits my nostrils. I quickly put my foot between the diaper and one of the dogs running toward it, attracted by the same odor, instinctually interesting to her.

"No, Shooggie, no!" I call out and she slides to a halt, her snout crashing into my calf. She withdraws with a sulk, turning once to double-check that the attractive-to-her smelling object remains off limits.

"I wish you were here, Mamma," I say, swallowing the lump in my throat.

"I do, too, my flower" she answers, and then quickly reminds me of the many international conferences she must attend in the next few months. My mom started her career in the 1960s as a secretary and then was head-hunted and trained to become a market analyst for one of Norway's largest maritime shipping companies. Now she holds this advanced position as the only woman among male industry leaders. She is proud of her accomplishments, and normally I am proud of her as well, but today I just want a doting, selfless mom.

"I also have a golf-trip planned to Mauritius with the ladies from my golf club next month, and then a tournament at the most scenic golf-course in Norway!"

I imagine her tanned and smiling, winning trophies, hitting birdies, and enjoying her gin and tonic at the 19th hole, surrounded by men who admire the gusto their wives don't have.

"I'm sooo tired," I say, "and Dan works pretty much seven days a week and comes home late at night most of the time." My voice cracks and I sniffle into the receiver.

Holding the baby's tummy with one hand I bend to pick up the dirty diaper from the floor; my fingers accidentally slip into the now cold and wet poop. Benya begins to squirm, I begin to sweat again, and I hear his brothers squabble in the den, accompanied by Big Bird and Cookie Monster singing their fucking happy song on TV. The dogs bark at something outside—their acute hearing their biggest (pain-in-the-ass) asset. Waves of nausea provoked by the stench of my own unbathed pits and shit-covered fingers roll through me, at the same time as a deep longing for my family in Norway overwhelms me. The now morose me slumps to the floor, holding the happy, gurgling chubster-baby close. I begin to sob. With my back against the cold, metal washer, Benya immediately roots for his mid-morning snack, and I oblige, lifting my breast-milk-stained jersey to let him have his fill, again. His warmth normally comforts me, but in this moment all I notice is my loneliness.

"Well, my gold nugget," Mom begins, one of her usual monikers for me making me even more emotional since it reminds me that I too, am somebody's child, "nobody said it was going to be easy to have three little ones so close."

I yearned for my mom's voice to soothe me, to tell me that these early years with starting a family are always the most difficult. I wanted her to comfort me by assuring me that energy, order, and manageability will return in my life soon enough; that she is proud of me. I wished she could have said, "Take a deep breath, my flower, and let me treat you to a massage or a mani-pedi and let me see if I can take some time off from work soon, to come to America and help you."

I could have called my mother-in-law, Joyce, a true *yiddishe mame* who lived an hour away and was both willing and able to help, since she was a homemaker who could not wait to get her hands on her grandchildren, my sons being her first precious three. She was always generous with her time, but she was not my mother. She understood and encouraged all things Jewish surrounding our family, but while her selfless devotion was something I both benefitted from and enjoyed (the food, the hugs, the availability!), it was also very different from anything with which I was familiar. I missed the way my mom smelled; I wanted to breathe in her Shalimar perfume and be comforted by *her*, not my mother-in-law.

Looking back, I see myself suspended—stretched even—between the ideals of my career-oriented, busy and, I imagined, fulfilled Scandinavian mom, and my family oriented Jewish-American mother-in-law who'd sacrificed her professional training as a physical therapist to be a homemaker. Each represented a certain version of what it meant to be a women, wife, mother, and daughter. To be secular and to be Jewish. I found myself conflicted by the two extreme role models that showed me ways to be, neither showing me my way. I had to forge my own path, and it was emotionally lonely at times. My mother didn't always appreciate my mother-in-law's choices, and vice versa.

Meanwhile, my life pulled me in a much more traditional direction than I ever imagined it would. I've wondered a whole lot what "pulled" or pushed me.

It seemed as though the ethos of "a traditional life" seeped into my being despite myself. Despite being raised by a feminist, career-oriented and financially independent mother, I was fully on-board when shaping my traditional (and patriarchal) Jewish life with Dan. I grew up in apartments in Oslo, the capital of Norway, and here I was, a young woman with three wee ones, moving into a gargantuan villa in suburbia, so cavernous that guests got lost between staircases and floors, entries and exits. This is where I wanted to be and become everything my mother was not.

Our new home was built in 1917 with a third floor to house a full staff as it did back in the origin days. We bought the house in 1998 (when the boys were almost four, almost two, and four months old), and the realtor told us that, in the 1920s, the family who lived here had not only servants lodged on the third floor, but a driver, a cook, and a gardener, too. When friends came over to check out our new digs, we'd playfully push the servant buzzers located on walls throughout the formerly grand house, and we'd all laugh at how nobody showed up. When I brought out and served drinks, we'd joke that *I* was the staff, but to me, this was not a joke at all.

My marriage and life had turned into an uber-traditional— or was it retrograde?—Jewish-American and gender-role segregated incubator, (think *Mad Men*) and it was all my own doing: I had played an active role in enabling that environment. A carefully crafted stage-set, I had been thirsty for a domestic setting different from the one I was raised in. I had wanted a marriage not like that of my parents, where my mom was the one with a regular and dependable salary, and my dad, too generous for his own good, was the nurturer who often floundered financially through various unsuccessful business projects. When faced with the rules and practicalities of a responsible adult life, where he had to pay bills and respect tax-laws, he failed dismally. I never really made a conscious choice, but I had married a parsimonious tax accountant, after all.

It was my creation, this domesticity and spousal arrangement that overwhelmed me as much as I wanted it. In their own way, then, my pale blue-ish stretch marks, the uneven pattern of bars in their parallel organization, ensure that the story of my pregnancies and maternal exhaustion remains written on my body. That the years in this glorious mansion that I turned into a more relaxed, colorful, and bohemian dwelling for raising a pack of wolf-cub-boys—as full and fulfilling as those years were— remains a time inscribed on my flesh.

What are the life-marks on our skin if not what bears witness to our past—the white scar on a woman's knee that reminds her of a fall off a bike, the blue tattoo on a sailor's arm that tells the tale of his ports of call (or the "MOM" that gave him life), the faded numbers on the Holocaust survivors forearm that whisper, *you will never forget.*

When I told my dear childhood friend Anne I was writing about my stretch marks, she said, "I *love* and strut my huge scar from my C-section! I'm proud of it!" Thanks to her, the marks on our skin suddenly become medals of achievement, these scars from the ordinary life battles we have survived. Our bodies, our skin, our storybooks: wars and victories, sorrows and joys, all inscribed there and connecting us to our memories, to our stories, and to ourselves. And to our meaning.

Teeth

Tonight, once more, life sinks its teeth
into my heart.
Simone de Beauvoir, *Tête-à-Tête*

There's a loud knock on our classroom door. We are twenty-three third graders sitting at our small, ergonomic desks at the Majorstuen School in Oslo, Norway, a large and gracious city building in cream-colored stucco dating from 1913. It is 1974. We are deep in the quiet exercise of taking dictation, and, while some kids pay attention, I am not among them.

"I think it's the dentist!" I instinctively blurt out. Miss Halstensen, our old spinster teacher with silvery, horned-rimmed glasses propped on her dainty nose, glares at me from her desk in front of the vast blackboard.

"I saw him going to the class next door before lunch!" I call again.

My classmates shrink or stir at their desks while a murmur mixed with dread and excitement sounds. We are nine years old and ready to welcome anything—even a visit from the much-feared school dentist and his dutiful assistant—that interrupts dictation in the slow-moving hours after lunch before our daily 2:30 p.m. dismissal. Sometimes the dental pair came to our classroom to call out a name, which meant it was that student's turn for an annual check-up. The state provided free dental care to children in a dental office located in a separate wing of our school building, near the nurse's office. This predictable check-up usually happened around the student's birthday, but for those of us with birthdays during summer vacation, like me, it was a wild card when we'd be called out.

What if it's my turn? I feel the rush of adrenaline running through me, and it's impossible to sit still. *Did I remember to brush my teeth this morning or did I sneak off to school having faked it, again?* I did run the faucet in the bathroom, swoosh water around in my mouth … But brush? I was a specialist sneak, and my parents never checked. My cheeks blush hot in anticipation of being caught in my toothbrushing lies by the boss of the toothbrushing police. If you were the unlucky kid whose name was called, it meant guaranteed torture from the unyielding school dentist and his merciless minion, the kind that left many of us traumatized for life, with lingering issues concerning all things dental.

It didn't occur to me that my exclamations disrupted the order of things. "Nina speaks out of turn; Nina interrupts …" my report cards read throughout elementary school. This was long before it was common to label, diagnose, and medicate kids with ADHD. I was the kid who flailed her arms to stay afloat all the way through elementary and middle school, until I learned how to compensate and self-censor in order to better fit in and to please.

The heavy, wooden classroom door painted a pale green with decorative beaded trim, opens slowly, and sure enough, it *is* the school dentist in his white frock, carrying a foot-and-a-half long red plastic toothbrush and a set of glistening fake teeth the size of a melon—uppers and lowers with lots of pink, shiny gums—followed by his assistant. She carries a tray with small, white plastic cups and a bottle labeled *Fluoride*. It is time for our bi-annual fluoride rinse and brushing lesson.

I think this ritual takes place in our classroom, but some of my girlfriends have told me we were usually escorted in an orderly file through the school hallways to a large room near the dentist's office. Pale-blue linoleum floors lined the hallways, and walls painted in soft yellow made the corridor cheery and disarmed the ominous sense that we were being led to our certain doom.

We were convinced the dentist's and doctor's offices were located far away from our classrooms so that nobody could hear the screams and moans escaping from sessions of poking, drilling, pulling, and other unimaginable torments. The school dentist was known to be heavy-handed, generous with the now-understood-to-be poisonous silvery amalgam fillings, and never used anything to dull the pain of the whining, spinning drill as he bore into our sensitive teeth and psyches, all the while scolding us for getting cavities.

For our fluoride rinse, the boys and girls stand in the shape of a horseshoe, laughing nervously, pointing at the spitting bucket on the floor in the middle of the room. The dentist stands at the opening of the horseshoe and demonstrates with slow and exaggerated hand movements the method for proper teeth brushing, the gigantic toothbrush looking comical.

"From the top and down, from the bottom and up, and then all the surfaces, and repeat," he instructs again and again.

We imitate his hand movements in front of our mouths amidst giggles, while the assistant hands out the cups with the fluoride. We are instructed to pour the contents into our mouths and to swish it around for what seems like an eternity. Inevitably, one or two kids snicker or clown around enough that they begin to squirt out some of the liquid, which dribbles down clothing to splatters on the floor, prompting others to have to hurry to the bucket before spewing the magic potion in each and every direction. On the verge of this circus, Miss Halstensen reprimands the culprits.

My memory of these days is different than what my friends recall for one specific reason: my father intervened to have me sit out from the fluoride treatments. I may have been part of the ritual only once or twice, instead of bi-annually throughout all elementary and middle school because my father was eager to guard our family against what he saw as the bureaucratic, socialist State dictating what should be done to his children. ("Communists," I heard him grumble). An autodidact and avid reader of everything, and especially science magazines, he understood fluoride as an unsafe substance, and felt that the preventative care imposed on school children (by the controlling State apparatus) did not outweigh the dangers of introducing the poison into our bodies. He wrote a letter to the principal when I was in middle school, demanding I be excused from the fluoride rinsing-sessions. His intention may have been to protect his little Nina, but in the end, it made me feel different and deprived, when all I wanted was to be like, and with, everybody else.

My father was *not* a socialist, and he was skeptical—to say the least—of any official mandates, including everything from seatbelt laws to the steep income taxes in our social welfare state, and of the heavy taxes on alcohol and cigarettes. Consequently, he received regular traffic violation tickets (rarely paid, piled high beneath the floor mat on the passenger side of his car, together with countless other unpaid bills and collection notices), evaded and protested personal income taxes (and eventually served time in jail for this "white-collar" crime), and was an avid bootlegger (in our basement wet room, where large, semitransparent plastic cans held the gin and vodka to be sold at below-market prices to friends and acquaintances who stopped by after dark—anything to save some *kroners* and defy the greedy, power-hungry State machinery). I imagine it gave him a sense of control and satisfaction vis-à-vis the government to be able to demand his daughter not be treated like part of a powerless herd.

And what was he saving me from? It's not as if my childhood years included any excellent or even regular dental home care. I stood in the tiny, warm bathroom in our apartment and faked my brushing; did a quick and careless swooshing of the toothbrush in my mouth, turning the faucet on to give the impression I was doing more than a mindless sweep. I felt clever, content that I managed to make my parents believe I brushed the way they wanted me to, the way I knew I should. Consequently, soon enough, cavities marked my molars, and the dark, silvery, cross-like shapes replaced one creased, enameled but browning and compromised surface after another.

Each time I sat in the reclining chair at the school's dentist office, the dentist's mask-less face so close to mine I could smell his sour breath, the shame was as painful if not deeper than that of the drill grinding its way deep into each tooth's softer, inner nerve-tissue. The smell of enamel smoldering into dust under the rotating metal bit is still with me, and the visceral feeling of the mercury mixture being packed bead by bead with a squeaky grind into the hollowed-out tooth gives me the shivers.

My friend Anette told me she was given "preventative fillings" in her entire mouth, which required a long and painful process of "de-amalgamization" later in life. Another friend, Christine, said her parents had heard so many horror stories about the public dentistry that they sent her to a private practitioner. My generation in Norway was certainly not blessed with dentist visits like the afternoon love fests my own kids enjoyed in the States, some thirty years later: a super-friendly dental staff greeting them in a bright, toy-filled waiting room with happy music softly playing in the background, a TV screen complete with video games and the latest Pixar or Disney videos, a choice of cherry-or bubblegum-flavored mouthwash, Novocain to numb the pain if any drilling was called for, and funny goggles to protect against the glare of the dental lamp. And, of course, a prize at the end of the visit. No dentist trauma for these kids.

.

On a balmy July night in 2009, after I had returned from a year in Norway with the kids to spend time with my dad who had just recovered from lung cancer, my husband and I were out for dinner at one of our favorite restaurants, Max's Oyster Bar.

I was savoring a piece of medium-rare, broiled salmon topped with house-made mango chutney, plated with roasted broccoli rabe and garlic mashed potatoes; a glass of Pinot Grigio sat in front of me on top a crisp, white tablecloth. Dan sat across from me, a rum and Coke in his hand, linguine with white clam sauce in front of him. A small candle flickered next to a budvase holding a singular orchid arching gracefully to one side. Sexy jazz music made the hum of a full house of diners seem less interfering to what I had hoped would be our intimate date night.

We had been struggling to get along for quite some time, especially since my return from Norway. This dinner date back in the States was another attempt at creating space for us without our three middle-school age kids around, and a time to talk and reconnect. Perhaps we could rediscover the good in that charming and gregarious person each of us fell so deeply in love with twenty-four years ago, when I was a fearless and braless Norwegian au pair, and he was a recent college graduate, working summers at Strawberry Park Campground in the rural, eastern corner of Connecticut where my host family and I spent Memorial Day weekend. Could we return to the summer of 1985, when Dan's six-foot-four-inch wide and muscular frame, dark complexion, and playful personality made my knees go weak?

It was my hope that we would weather this marital bump in the road to what I assumed would be a long, dedicated life together, since I never imagined divorce as an option. But Dan did not agree to us seeking marriage counseling. "They are all kooks," he'd say with a shrug when I suggested we find someone. "The reason they become therapists is because they are crazy themselves."

During that memorable dinner he looked up from his linguine cooked *al dente* and focused on my mouth as if he was about to tell me something sweet, perhaps even sexy, like he used to. Instead, he motioned with his finger toward his own front teeth, his lips parting in a forced smile, his teeth small for such a big man. Pushing his chin forward, as if to demonstrate the urgency and location of my problem, he said, "You've got some green stuck between your lateral incisor and right cuspid."

"I am actually still chewing, so maybe the minutiae of dental appearance can wait until I am done eating?" My words slipped out with more sarcasm than I intended, and something stung, inside me. Disappointment; both at his unromantic and OCD comment, and my own reactive response. I had always joked that if Dan and his family were as obsessed with their emotional hygiene as they were with their oral hygiene, it would benefit everyone. But it wasn't a joke, really.

My father-in-law was a highly acclaimed oral surgeon, and judging teeth seemed to be my in-law clan's way of evaluating people. Visible plaque or missing teeth were quickly deemed as character flaws. The wisest and warmest community rabbi was disdained if his oral hygiene was regarded below par, and a piece of food stuck between your incisors had to be immediately removed; it was code red. Raw onions or garlic were avoided at all costs because of the bad breath factor.

I have always loved onions and will *schmear* the nutty content of an entire roasted head of garlic on bread, pizza, or pasta. During my marriage to Dan, I snuck garlic into Chicken Marbella, pasta sauces, stir fried veggies and salad dressings, knowing my dishes would be blissfully devoured by all who sat around my table, even my husband. If Dan asked if the undesired ingredient was present, I muttered "no," and between mouthfuls and *Yum!*, and *Ooh!*, and *Ah!*, he seemed quite content. Perhaps I was the one who set the stage for betrayal.

Dan once told me that one of the things that attracted him

to me, aside from the bralessness and blondness, were my "nice teeth." But that night, out in our favorite restaurant for a much-longed-for date-night, with a spec of broccoli rabe sullying my smile, my tarnished teeth became a metaphor for how he saw me. All that stands out to me from that evening is my urgent wish to make our time together matter. I had put on an outfit that made me feel sexy and was eager to rouse that palpable energy and carefree humor we shared, that so many times had swooped us closer together emotionally. Instead, my teeth became the object of deflection during what seemed to me a critical moment, so vivid in my body.

Not long after that evening out, Dan and I agreed that the impasse of our relationship was unbearable, his unwillingness to work on our marriage devastating me. Eventually, I would discover photos on his iPhone of a woman with much bigger and whiter teeth than mine. With no broccoli rabe in sight.

This was the time in my life when I had recurring nightly dreams of losing my teeth. I would wake filled with horror at the uncannily vivid awareness and taste of spitting out one hard, enameled lump after another—*pthuh, pthuh, pthuh*—teeth that no longer stayed attached to my bones and gums. Irregularly shaped pearls with a jagged, red edge landing pell-mell and shiny in the palm of my hand. What could it possibly mean? In the dreams I run panicked into the dentist office, hysterically pleading with them to *do something!*

From the Internet I soon learned that dreams about losing teeth can be understood as a sign of insecurity and ambivalence. That fear of our teeth falling out is our subconscious telling us about the great cost of inaction or compromise when we are not being true to ourselves. Our teeth are so precious to us that the image of losing them arbitrarily and dramatically in dreams suggests at some level we understand what's really happening in our lives.

Teeth are also our primal defense, and I must have felt utterly defenseless, as if all my earlier held assumptions about my life's security and protection were not just threatened but being snapped off at the roots. Add to that the fact that teeth help keep us alive, masticating and making our foods digestible, and I had all the more to fear in the dreams of losing these parts of my body, so crucial to survival.

Biologically, our teeth are parts of us that remain intact long after death; in a sense they are the last proof of our individual existence. In light of this morbid but natural fact, it's easy to imagine how impending divorce represented a profound existential threat for me; its own death. What I didn't understand then, thinking in horror about my dental nightmares, was that like teeth that remain intact after death, I too would be able to not only survive, but endure strong and resilient after the inevitable demise of my marriage.

Hair

A woman who cuts her hair
is about to change her life.
Coco Chanel

In my first-day-of-school photo from 1972, I am a flaxen-haired girl with a short pixie cut, cute little sideburns outlining my still-chubby cheeks. I am wearing a white-and-blue-striped, short dress and white knee highs, and in the picture from that day, barely in color, the reds and blues of the clothing and the green of the trees are washed out and distant as if part of a hazy dream. My classmates and I are all comically towheaded, as if the photographer had ordered up identical, Scandinavian six-year-olds for the representative shoot.

My backpack resembles all the other backpacks that my new friends and first graders carry: rectangular, plaid, and boxy; this is an era long before ergonomic design has hit the industry. I'm carrying it a little crooked on my back and the thin, white leather straps make the backpack seem empty, except for the brand-new pencil case that I know rattles inside.

We stand in front of the small, round fountain in the center of the stucco-walled schoolyard. Of all those lined up in a semi-circle that day, aside from a redhead named Ingrid, only one of the girls is a brunette. Her name is Tina and eventually we will learn that she was adopted, and what it means to be adopted.

In the photo I am almost a head taller than her and a giant next to her and many of the other girls' petite frames. When Tina told me her name and I told her mine, I thought "Nina" made me seem so boring, since it was one of the most common names around, several just in my class. I wished I had a name like Anastasia or Isabella, something different and exotic, and that Tina and I could become close friends, like those in the statue in the center of the schoolyard fountain with two children fashioned from bronze, lying side by side on their bellies, smiling, their feet up in the air, their gazes fixed into the shallow water surrounding them.

When I look at photos of myself as a child, I see a typical Norwegian girl who has no idea yet how much she is part of a homogenous community, and how much she will seek to break away from it as soon as she enters adolescence. As I mature into a teenager, I begin to feel like an outsider, despite the fact that I look the same as everyone else. Hair, I learn, can play a significant part of identity, and this I decide to experiment with.

.

One day, in high school, I showed up with voluminous, blonde hair, having paid handsomely for a full perm with my hard-earned money from several regular afterschool jobs. My normally long, straight locks hadn't differentiated me from how most girls wore their hair at the time, and the new hairdo appealed to my newly acquired aesthetic: less conforming, more individualistic. Sure, girls got perms in those days, but none of my peers sported the shorter, plump variety that framed my round, red cheeks and blue eyes that winter in 1983. This hair experiment certainly didn't have the effect of integrating me more into the student body, but it did bestow me with a certain sense of audaciousness for braving to stand out in the crowd. While I sought out this "difference," I still remember the sting of being an outsider who never quite fit in, and I was acutely aware of this contradiction, always. At this stage, my classmates knew I preferred reggae clubs instead of David Bowie and Duran Duran, and Black and Brown (older) boyfriends to the milky white, immature peers, from my school. "Somebody's got jungle fever!" I'd hear behind my back during recess. Yeah, this was a thing people said in the early eighties.

Instead of hanging out with my classmates and peers, I spent most of my time after school and on weekends working, or training horses at the Oslo Equine Center. My many hours at the stables didn't bring me cash but free rides on a variety of gorgeous equine creatures and hanging out in this milieu also marked the beginning of a friendship that opened up an entirely different world to me.

Diedra, one of the lucky few teens who owned her own horse, was a chestnut-haired half Norwegian, half American (and quarter Native American) girl that I spent a lot of time with, both in and out of the stables. This was a phase of self-discovery for us, and at sixteen years old, she introduced me to social circles where the average ethnic Norwegian teenager in the early 1980s was not known to hang out.

Diedra's boyfriend, Mike, was from Trinidad, and his family and friends were our portal into immigrant circles. There, Diedra and I explored reggae-infused nightclubs, concerts, and home parties in Oslo neighborhoods where our families and friends did not normally venture; we smoked pot—not as common in Norway then as in the US—and attended large gatherings where food and music were organized by members of the various immigrant communities from North Africa, the Caribbean, and Sub-Saharan Africa. A few ethnic Norwegians were present, almost always women, like us. Often, the young men in each immigrant sub-group seemed suspicious of their peers from other countries; the Gambians did not always appreciate the Jamaicans, who did not think the Tunisians were trustworthy, who thought the Pakistanis were prudish and had a chip on their shoulder for being the oldest immigrant group of Black and Brown people, and so the various ethnic groups often remained segregated.

Diedra and I schemed plenty and deftly navigated this teenage phase together, the way girlfriends are in cahoots and gain (not always wise) bravery in pairs, pushing parental boundaries by staying out past curfews, lying about where we spent the night and whom we were with, while exploring our budding sexuality.

What does this have to do with hair you might wonder? As psychologist Vivian Diller points out, we are likely hardwired to feel emotionally connected to our hair, and it's no secret that *hair* is seen as a powerful indicator of *identity*. So, bear with me, reader, because the beauty of mining our body for memories is that once a particular part starts to lead you down a road to remembrance, interconnected pathways will pop up. Together, they help shape a fuller picture of how your life experiences have shaped the unique you. Thinking about my hair swept me down my identity-finding-path, and wait until you see what else this will lead to. To some pretty repressed shit (as in experiences), that's where.

Mike, who was a few years older than us, maybe twenty-one, had shoulder-length, wavy black hair that framed his Indian features, and a great smile with big, healthy, and bright-white teeth. His cheeks were pockmarked, and his nose rounded, but this didn't detract from how good-looking we considered him: he was fit and his butt looked great in his red-tab Levi's. He had a great sense of humor, so we laughed a lot when we hung out with him and his much older friend Julien, to whom I took a liking, and vice versa.

Trinis are typically a mix, both racially and culturally, of people from Africa, India, and China, as well as white Europeans, and Mike spoke English with a sing-songy accent that he combined with words from his native patois. Julien, from Mauritius—the island in the Indian Ocean with much of the similar ethnic mix as in Trinidad and known for its magnificent diversity and tolerance among its population—was in his thirties, twice my age. The black-haired, Brown men we hung out with, lived and socialized mostly downtown and on the east side of Oslo, in the traditionally working-class neighborhoods, where many immigrants found affordable rentals.

With my new "blonde fro" hairdo and wearing a rose-colored 1980s silk pantsuit I had bought but hidden from my parents, Diedra and I hit the nightclub at one of the hotels downtown. I felt mature and excited when smooth-talking Julien showed interest in me and bought me drinks. His mixed Afro-Asian heritage made him intriguing to me, and he wore his kinky, black hair close-cropped. I loved that he spoke fluent French, Italian *and* Norwegian, in addition to English and Creole; the way he held his cocktails, and the way the cigarette smoke slowly snaked up and around his face. On the dancefloor, our hips slowly ground to the seducing rhythms and lyrics of Barry White and Marvin Gaye; it was sexual healing all the way home.

When Julien spoke English, which was the language our gang always bantered in, he did it with a Jamaican accent, heavily laced with resonances of the playful and earthy patois that makes West Indies Creole distinct; he was a man with a truly mixed cultural and linguistic background. Julien worked at the *Instituto Italiano di Cultura* in Oslo where he was a receptionist. This was not a typical immigrant job in the early eighties, since most positions other than menial jobs (and consular jobs, like his) would require near fluency in Norwegian. This was also before the fall of the Berlin Wall in 1989, and globalization as we know it today had not yet become part of everyday parlance. English was not yet the typical go-to language heard widely in the service industry in Norway, the way it is today, especially in the capital.

Julien' job allowed him to carry on as a bit of a dandy, sporting silk scarves and elegant leather shoes, although he was anything but well off, living in a one-room studio with a dingy toilet in the building's public stairwell, the kind of loo with a wooden handle pull-string dangling from a porcelain tank suspended on the wall above the bowl. The entrance to his place was from the courtyard of a turn-of-the-twentieth-century low-rise, commercial, city building, where discarded cartons and crates overflowed from a huge, grimy container in the narrow driveway. But his building was in a more desirable part of town, and his street well-known for all the unique shops.

I wonder now if he adopted the West Indies accent because his buddies were all from the Caribbean, and if he too yearned to fit in, in some ways like I did. Our casual relationship lasted for about a year, and for me it was more about sexual awakening and typical teen exploration of boundaries and freedom than anything romantic. I would invent all sorts of deceptions to spend the night at his place without my parents knowing, like telling my parents I was staying at Diedra's house.

But they did eventually find out about him and our little love nest because one early morning, my mother rang his doorbell. My blue moped parked outside the entrance must have been a dead give-away. When Julien opened the door, I could hear from under the covers that she asked if I was there, her voice sounding terse. I sheepishly stepped up to the open threshold—all of three steps from his bed—cheeks flushed in embarrassment. All she said in a flat voice was, "You should come home now." There was an absence of words and a crushing sense of shame in facing both my mother and Julien, but perhaps mostly in facing myself.

She never talked about the incident, except on a rare occasion—maybe once or twice in total—when I was older, and we would reminisce about my "rebellious years." She'd refer to it as "that time I had to come get you from that guy on Hegdehaugs Street." Well, that guy had a name, and it was Julien, and I would get pregnant by him the spring I was seventeen.

Kaboom: thinking about how my hair played a role in my evolving teen identity brought me to my sexual awakening which happened in the immigrant community in Oslo, which brought me here, to my teen pregnancy, which I have not thought a whole lot about ... Until I do, now.

In April 1983, my mother and I went on a week-long charter vacation to the island of Ibiza, where my skin was (again) singed to a crisp, this time under the alluring Mediterranean sun. I had surprised her with tickets because between my frequent work gigs I had a fat bank account for a teen. I'm guessing I was trying to get on her good side again, especially after the awkward confrontation in the door opening of Julien' tiny studio.

The getaway to the Spanish island known for its white beaches and debauchery was a steal and included the flight and six nights at a three-star hotel. Mom offered to pay for all the other expenses, which I'm sure must have run much more than what I had paid for the bargain package deal. We had a great time: aside from the requisite sunburns, we pranced around the island, a beaming mother-daughter power team of towering Scandinavian and blonde femaleness with all the connotations this meant for the locals (easy-going, fun, loud, uninhibited …). We hit the dancefloors of dark and steamy nightclubs where Michael Jackson's *Thriller* album was all the rage. "Billie Jean" made us scream with joy and run to the disco-lighted parquet floors, sipping umbrella drinks, flirting wildly, and practicing our Spanish with grinning, handsome waiters while waving off dull German and drunk British admirers.

However, during our week on sandy beaches in the bright sun, steering clear of the safe shade offered by palm trees and beach umbrellas, I noticed that the period I was expecting didn't come.

I realized I might be pregnant. I never told my mother this—if she or my dad suspected it, they never said anything—and I also postponed going to the clinic until later in the summer, meaning I ended up having an abortion past the twelfth week. Aside from the doctors at the state-run clinic, Diedra was the only person in the universe whom I had told about the pregnancy. I did not even tell Julien because for some reason, I assumed all the responsibility. I was ashamed. *Had I been a dumb blonde, after all?* With a curious detachment, as if moving in a tunnel where there was only one way out, I remained strangely calm and collected throughout the ordeal, which at the time was not much of an ordeal at all but an inconvenient detour as a result of what I saw as my carelessness. In other words, major repression of emotions while going through a pretty disturbing and lonely experience.

At some point soon after the abortion, Mike told Diedra that Julien had another girlfriend, Marilyn, also from Mauritius, who had gotten pregnant several times by him. Each pregnancy had been terminated, and hearing this, I felt grossed out by him, probably intensified by regret of my own reckless behavior. Today I understand this as a projection of how I really felt about myself. I knew about birth control; it's even possible he asked me about it to be responsible, and looking back I don't understand why I didn't protect myself. I think I may even have lied to him and said not to worry, that I was on the pill. I wanted to appear cool and in control. I didn't want to seem like the young, inexperienced woman I was.

My parents—strangely—never talked to me about the importance of birth control or any "what if" scenarios. I say strangely, since this was "liberal" Scandinavia and they were partiers and not morally or religiously against sex before marriage; after all, I was conceived three months before my parents were married. But for some reason, although their oldest daughter stayed out late and night and sleeping over at "friends," it never came up.

On a rainy weekend at the tail end of the summer when my parents were away, I drove my moped to the hospital where the abortion was to take place. I had spent the entire summer living and working at the seaside resort owned by my dad's best friend and had hoped (what was I thinking?) the pregnancy would terminate itself. Go away. Disappear. I was working so hard, toiling in manual labor all around the resort compound, wouldn't that increase the chances of a natural miscarriage? Needless to say, it was magical thinking that did not work. Instead, the fetus took hold in what was my seventeen-year-old hyper-fertile and healthy womb—biologically the ideal spot and time; realistically, not so much.

I don't recall much from the hours I spent at the hospital that day. The visuals in my mind's eye are constructed from various abortion narratives I have read and seen in films since. I don't trust the few flickering images of waiting and recovery rooms I can conjure as being mine, or as being real. When I woke up from the anesthesia, after a brief period of recovery, I was instructed to go home and rest, so I did. The staff told me to take a taxi and that I should pick up my moped in a day or two. When I developed bad cramps and a fever in the evening, I blamed myself, and was convinced I would never be able to have children. Curled in a fetal position in my parents' empty bed, I called Diedra; she picked up a prescription and by the next day I felt better.

I tucked the experience of my teenage abortion neatly into a corner of my mind and body where I didn't have to pay much attention to it until I was married and had trouble conceiving. Each time I discovered the bloody spots that signaled another period in lieu of the much-desired pregnancy, I thought, *there you go, serves you right for your careless behavior of unprotected teenage sex.* And each time I've had to fill out the medical history form at the OB-GYN's, I've included the abortion under "how many pregnancies have you had?"—my answer: four—but continued to feel strangely removed from it, as if the experience didn't really belong to me. To the next question, "How many children do you have?" (or do they ask about "live births"?), my answer has always been three. None of this included the early miscarriage I had during my fertility treatment in my late twenties: a four-week-old gelatinous mass of blood and cells that didn't quite fit down the drain in the shower, where it landed heavy after sliding out of me. I never knew where this event belonged with the definitions of numbers of pregnancies.

I think I never made room for or gave myself permission to mourn and truly process any of these events; not the abortion when I was seventeen, nor the miscarriage when I was twenty-eight. On a rare occasion I've wondered about what my mixed-ethnicity child would have looked like, and a few times I've caught myself calculating how old he or she would have been in a given year. Briefly, my mind might wander to imagine how my life would have been different had I not terminated the pregnancy...

Shortly after my abortion, the relationship with Julien ended. I just stopped seeing him; as far as I can recall, there was no drama or ambiguity from either end, which was fine because for me it was about experimentation, excitement, not love. And as it is with experiments, knowledge was acquired, and lessons learned. Later that fall, Diedra and I made our first appointment at the Norwegian version of Planned Parenthood.

I sit on a low stool in my Gambian boyfriend Edi's narrow kitchen as his cousin Assia braids my hair into dozens of tight and detailed cornrows. It's a Saturday, specifically February 18, as Edi and his friends and family are celebrating their homeland's freedom from British colonialism. Assia wears a colorful Gambian dress in honor of their celebration; long and loose, it has a bold print in greens, browns, and orange, and her hair is braided elaborately, close to her scalp in a circular parallel halo, with a tight collection of long, thin, black braids nestled neatly in the nape of her neck. At this point my hair is long, straight and naturally blond, but I am far from a towhead anymore. The braids of the African women in my new boyfriend's circle mesmerize me; I love how their hair is such an intricate and stunning expression of their cultural belonging and identity.

"They are beautiful!" I had said to him as we looked at photos of his female family members, a few weeks before.

"You can have braids, too," he said, looking at me with a warm smile, twirling a strand of my hair between his fingers. "My cousin braids professionally and she'll be here next week for the party I'm throwing for Gambia's Independence Day."

While Assia works methodically through my thick hair and I occasionally twitch or cringe when she accidentally pulls too hard, we are mostly silent in our complicity. I notice the way she smells; a sweet mix of the incense from the cotton fabric of her dress, and what I think is ylang ylang and shea butter from her skin. I wonder if she thinks I have a particular odor. In an interview with immigrants from Pakistan in a Norwegian magazine, one woman pointed out that as much as her blond and pale fellow landsmen readily remark that the new Norwegians smell like pungent curry, the woman and her fellow Pakistanis laugh about how ethnic Norwegians' skin emanates the rancid stink of sour milk and dairy products. So there. The interview made me smile, and I enjoyed showing the article to my conservative parents, who often expressed negative views about immigrants' seeming unwillingness to assimilate and "change their ways." "When in Rome do as the Romans," I heard them say.

Somebody takes a picture of Assia and me in the kitchen that day that I will later glue into my photo album from 1984, when I'm a senior in high school. At the celebratory gathering this particular occasion, all are Gambians except me. While it takes Assia over four hours to finish braiding my hair, the delicious meat stews *demachin* and *domoda* simmer on the stove next to me, spreading moist and fragrant air throughout the apartment. Edi, his family and friends speak Wolof to each other, and a mix of English and Norwegian with me, or when I'm in the room.

Edi and I met at the reggae club Diedra and I frequented, where the majority of the patrons were Black and Brown, non-European immigrants like Mike, Julien, and Edi. Sweaty bodies swaying and hips grinding on the small, crowded, and dark dancefloor to the hypnotic beats of Bob Marley, Black Uhuru, and Peter Tosh, our hungry body-language expressed itself without words. Edi and I began dating in the winter of my eighteenth year, and on New Year's Eve of 1983/84, we sat across from each other at Velente's Italian restaurant, a popular romantic joint in Oslo. We sipped red wine over the flickering flame of a red candle propped into a repurposed, oval and straw-based Chianti bottle, red wax dripping down its sides like hot lava. We gazed across the table with hunger and playful desire. At one point I let my boot drop to the floor under the table, and inched my foot toward Edi's crotch and moved it around with a mischievous smile. "You are a crazy woman," he said, and looked around the room, only to grab my foot under the table and press it harder against him. I relished that he called me a crazy woman.

Edi was blacker than black—almost blue. His body was slender and muscular, and the white of his eyes two small but bright moons, except when he was high, when they turned a mix of brownish red and yellow. He was much older than me—thirty-six to my eighteen. I loved going to his "grown up" place on the other side of Oslo from where I and my bourgeois parents lived. His one-bedroom apartment was spacious with a "manly" black leather sectional and black-lacquered furniture, colorful African wall hangings and incense burners in every room.

At home, he liked to wear a traditional kaftan or *jalabe*, and together we smoked pot and had sex on the floor in front of his glass-fronted living room wall unit, where, infatuated by our own reflections, we mused about the sharp contrast of my lean, white body on top of or underneath his black. "Look at us," I'd say, "isn't it beautiful?" and we'd both turn toward the shimmery image of entwined limbs and relish in the dramatic visual with smiles and kisses while reggae music thumped lazily in the background.

At the party when my hair was braided, I am the only ethnic Norwegian, but it doesn't bother me. I love the more raucous and lively mood, such a difference from my own home where you can hear the sound of our knives and forks hit the plates in the decorous mood of family dinners where nobody interrupts or laughs too loudly. I have sought out this setting where I am comfortable and where I can experience what it's like to be the minority, the one who is "other"—as if this is something I want to understand and feel. Or maybe I like it because it gives me a sense of being special; different than the majority culture of the ethnic Norwegians which I am part of, where I don't feel unusual at all, but rather just like a bland nobody in a sea of homogeneous, Scandinavian, fair-skinned sameness. Maybe it was the *attention* I yearned for; to be noticed, a way to feel seen was by putting myself in situations and milieus where I was the odd (wo)man out.

When I come home that night, all decked out in my African braids and probably reeking of both pot, incense, and foreign-smelling spices, I imagine my parents cringing, even though they never say anything. Despite being educated and well-travelled, their social world is what I have come to call a "mutual admiration society," in which they and their friends are more or less all from the same class, same ethnicity, same culture, and same conservative (that is, not socialist, not labor party, not union supporters) political views. Many of the guys are small business owners, like my father, a real *petite bourgeoisie.*

When Edi calls for me a few days later and my father answers the phone, his announcement is unforgettable: "Nina, it's for you," he calls out, and as he hands me the receiver (of the corded landline phone sitting on the desk in our living room) he adds, "it's a fellow who doesn't eat with a knife and fork." Edi's accent alerts my dad to his foreign origins, and my dad just can't resist the jab. To him, most Africans are barbarians, and since I have not yet learned about the toxic and delusional Western tradition of colonialist, imperialist (oh, and let's add Christian, white and male, for good measure) tropes of othering (my university studies in postcolonial literary criticism will open my eyes in more ways than one) I am not incensed by his attitude, but instead decide to repress my feelings of annoyance in the good stoic form in which I was raised.

However, I did write a letter to the editor of the period's iconic teen girls' magazine *Det Nye* (aimed at ages sixteen to twenty), complaining about my parents' xenophobia. The letter was published and signed "Virgo 1965." My father, the avid reader who'd devour everything written in sight (except our household utility bills and his personal tax documents), recognized my printed, anonymously signed letter. After knocking on my bedroom door, he poked his head in and held out the latest copy of my magazine subscription. "Is it you who wrote this?" he asked. The flash of heat in my face surely revealed my identity, so I answered "yes," and owned up to my written complaint.

I kept the braids in for a few weeks, turning heads at school and in the streets, some strangers complimenting me, others discreetly catching a second glance. This was the summer of 1984, right after I had graduated from high school, just before I flew to the US to be an *au pair* for a gap year between high school and university studies. The day before my departure, my friend Gørill comes over to help undo the braids. I'm seated on a tattered stool in the middle of my tiny bedroom off our kitchen, a room originally intended for the maid when our apartment building was built in "the olden days." Tears spring to my eyes as she tugs and pulls while untangling the tight and artful strands of hair, turned fuzzy and less neat in a matter of weeks. Clothes are scattered on the floor and on my bed. Two huge suitcases stand at attention under the window, waiting to be filled with a year's worth of clothing, and the feeling that an era is about to end is palpable, while the excitement of new beginnings fills my imagination. I am getting ready to leave my childhood home and city and country to live abroad for the first time—for what I think will be "just" one year.

.

When I've lived in the US for the better part of thirty-plus years, I again sit in front of a mirror at my hairdresser's salon, draped in a black satin smock, dozens of thin strips of foil paper folded over strands of my hair. I look ridiculous and avert my eyes from the garish reflection in the mirror. The chemicals sting my scalp and the skin around my hairline, but I tolerate it because I like the result: the golden streaks lift me up and somehow cement my identity as a Scandinavian, despite my accent that people tell me is faint if at all noticeable. *To cement my identity as a Scandinavian.*

Oh, the irony.

Hands

Through the red and blue strobing lights and low-seeping cloud of cigarette smoke, I take in the fat forty-something standing by the bar laughing with a bunch of men, all around his age—smug, entitled, boozed up. I run toward him from the side, my arm raised and my hand clenched. When I get within reach, I pull my fist back for maximum velocity and punch his jaw. Down he goes; it is a knockout of epic proportion. I am twenty-five and really, really pissed off.

A writing mentor once asked if I have ever used my hands to defend myself, and the answer is, *hell yeah*. It happened in Oslo, on a pleasantly warm summer evening in the early 1990s, when my best friend Anne and my sister Tone (*Tooneh*) and I were out on the town. We wanted to dance and have a few (more) drinks, and headed to the iconic nightclub Frascati, known to draw a more mature clientele. It was also the place to pick up high-end prostitutes, a fact I only learned later.

Frascati was on the second floor of an elegant commercial building downtown, and to access it, we had to go through the large, glass front doors, and then follow a grand, marble staircase to the dramatic entry of the club. Up we went in good spirits, all a little tipsy, the groovy rhythms of Motown hits bellowing throughout the building.

I was dressed in long, cream-colored palazzo pants, and a matching blazer with sheer, floral sleeves. I also wore pearl earrings; in all, it was an outfit that was uncharacteristically preppy and elegant relative to my usual bohemian style. A bouncer with bulging muscles asked for our IDs while a forty-something man with a paunch and business suit was greeted with smiles and sailed right through. *A regular guest,* I thought, miffed at the differential treatment. But, suddenly and before he disappeared through the curtains separating the club from the foyer, the man turned to me, a whiff of alcohol preceding him.

His eyes didn't quite focus as he leaned in, too close. "You look like a cheap hooker, you know that?" he said. Then he swung around and pranced through the heavy doorway draperies.

I was so stunned, I didn't even have a chance to respond, but a pang of adrenaline rushed through my body. The bouncer let us in, oblivious to the offense that had just taken place right in front of him. Barely inside, I spotted the asshole immediately through the smoke, my eyes narrow slits focusing in on his silhouette; I became an instant homing device on the tip of a charged torpedo.

That's when I punched the motherfucker. Before I had a chance to notice how the people standing around him reacted, I turned on my heels and ran out through the velvet drapes, anticipating an aggressive reaction. I flew down the majestic stairs, but the soles of my shoes slipped on the marble, and I landed on my butt, sliding down the rest of the hard stairs on my back. Bam, bam, bam-bam, down I went.

My sister and Anne followed behind, confused and squealing as we all ran outside. We tumbled together in a cluster on the sidewalk, breathless and cracking up while they asked me if I was okay, and what the heck just happened. The knuckles of my right hand ached and pulsated, and my heart pumped out of my chest. I hadn't hit anyone since I straddled Sverre Hustad in eighth grade and gave him a bloody nose for bullying a new kid in our class.

Just as we were catching our breath, the muscly bouncer barged through the front doors scowling, puffed up like a blowfish, heading straight toward us, fast. I reached into my purse for the bottle of mace that I had never used, but that I knew was in there somewhere. My American sisters-in-law had gifted it to me, concerned about me travelling alone without their brother, my husband. At the time, I had snickered internally at what I saw as their paranoia.

I pulled out the little handy-dandy spray bottle and aimed it in the bouncer's direction, fumbling to find the trigger. He was already so close that he managed to grab my wrist and bend my arm back, which made the fine mist of blinding agent change direction, straight into my face. I screamed in pain. Tone and Anne responded by jumping on his back, kicking and screaming. Before we knew it, a police van pulled up on the sidewalk next to us and two cops broke up the fight.

The three of us girls were escorted into the back of the black, ominous van while the officers kept the beefy bouncer outside, questioning him. That's when I noticed that my punching hand was bleeding and my back was in agony from the bumpy ride down the stairs. I also felt nauseous and had trouble breathing from the spray, and my eyes stung like hell. I was a mess, and the police decided to take us to the ER to have me checked out.

No charges were pressed and if anything, the cops and the ER staff seemed humored by my moxie, without saying it out loud. In later years, Anne, my sister and I have giggled at the doctor's notes, which we sneaked a peek at when he stepped out of the room: "Patient smells like ethanol," it said. Indeed, she did.

Much later, around 4 a.m., birds chirping and Oslo's mid-summer night sky already blue and bright, my sister and I crawled out of a taxi outside our parents' apartment building. We were exhausted but exhilarated and had a damn good story to tell our folks.

The next morning, with a white gauze bandage around my fist and open surface wounds along my spine, I hobbled into our sunny top-floor kitchen. There, smoking his usual ciga-rettes and sipping his coffee, our dad made us breakfast while we recounted the dramatic events of the night before. He smiled and laughed and told us he was proud of his girls for standing up to a man's insult. He later loved to tell guy friends about the Frascati incident of his daughters not taking shit from a guy, and in time the story took on mythic proportions. My three now-adult sons still love to hear it repeated today, how their mamma punched a slime bag.

With my hands, I sew buttons and hem curtains and make delicious meals and shovel snow. I paint walls and furniture, plant flowers and vegetables in our garden, and carry heavy groceries from the store.

My hands do laundry and iron and clean windows and floors and massage my beloved's feet and scratch his back. My hands and fingers collaborate with my mind and heart to write the stories I must tell.

I hold the door for the person behind me, and I hand over a home-made meal to a neighbor. But best of all is when my hands reach out to embrace those I love, and even, on occasion, a stranger.

.

There are scars. The middle finger on my left hand has a one-inch-long scar that dimples in slightly at the tip, diagonally from the nail down toward the pillowy part of the digit. It still feels numb to touch, more than twenty years after the incident that maimed it.

My three kids were all under the age of five, it was the time of day of the much-dreaded bewitching hour, when young'uns get tired, testy, and whiny, and I was home alone with them. And about to open a can of dog food. After I had turned the handle all the way around the top of the lid and I could tell it had loosened, I absentmindedly grabbed it by its edges and twisted. Our two Lhasa Apso pups who stirred by my feet were not the only hungry creatures in the kitchen. I let the boys snack on Goldfish to keep them busy until I finished with the dogs, but the snack bowl with the tiny, bright orange crackers fell to the floor, someone started crying, and Gabi ran from the kitchen, probably to escape the chiding he was used to provoking. Suddenly, the jagged lid slipped in my hand and an icy sensation ran from my skull down my spine through my feet. I looked down at my hand where a white tip of bone in my finger was visible.

Blood squirted, and I intuitively grabbed a nearby kitchen towel and wrapped it tight around the compromised digit. I realized I couldn't pack up the kids and drive to urgent care, so I called a friend who was an ER doctor and neighbor. Fortunately, he was home. Within a few minutes, Scott was in our kitchen with his vintage, leather doctor kit, and we were all standing over the kitchen sink he'd covered with a sterile, blue, paper square to prepare the "operating room." Before the stiches, he injected my finger with Novocain in several places. My face twitched and I took a couple of deep breaths to keep cool as the kids gathered around us, silent and in awe. The best entertainment ever!

"Mamma, are you okay?" Tobi asked, looking intently at the tip of the needle disappearing into my finger. Big-eyed and enthralled, he and his brothers followed the movements of Scott's hand as the needle and thread closed the wound with six stitches.

"I'm going to be fine," I assured him. "Aren't we lucky to have Scott right here? And check out how he's sewing my finger and it doesn't even hurt!" I added in a bit of a forced upbeat tone.

I was their hero, as was Scott, who saved their mamma's fingertip. I bought a new can-opener soon after; a fancy Swiss design that leaves the lid edges smooth to touch and will not harm a soul. If you can just figure out how to use it.

.

My hands have their own vivid muscle memory, especially of holding other hands. Like the firm, solid clutch of my youngest Benya's toddler hand in the fleshy grip of my palm. His natural independence meant that he wanted the holding to feel just so. On the contrary, Tobi didn't hold on much at all, so I had to be mindful to tighten my grip around his chubby hand, so it didn't slip from mine. Gabi could never get close enough. He clutched tightly whether it was with hands, legs, or all four. If I let go when he was not ready, everyone would hear about it.

They are no longer little boychiks but young adult men, yet their temperaments remain consistent. The good news for me is that they still all like to hold my hand.

The thrill of clutching fists with my sons in occasional arm-wrestle challenges as they grew into strong teenagers reverberates in my hand-memories. We would melt together in a sweaty grip as our faces turned red, moans and groans escaping our mouths until finally roars sounded as the winner crushed the loser's hand down on our imperfect wooden kitchen tabletop. Eventually the day arrived when one by one, they beat their mamma in the duel, and I had to dish out the promised dollars or coins or favor. Yummy days when my sons were all within a hand's reach.

The problem was that my ex-husband Dan's touch was always enough to renew my hope in *us*. During our separation, at a meeting mandated by the State of Connecticut for parents who were divorcing, it happened again. The carpeted conference room was half-filled with orderly rows of upholstered chairs, and some parents sat next to one another. Others—surely soured by the experience of breaking up—stayed far apart, trying hard not to look at one another, noses buried in their phones. Dan and I sat next to each other, our arms and legs touching. The energy in the room was guarded and toned-down, and only some participants chatted quietly, as we did.

I had already moved out of our house to my new condo down the street, and our boys were dividing their time between our two homes. During our year-long separation and divorce process, Dan and I hovered in an emotionally muddled in-between space, a sort of hellish purgatory where the push and pull of doubt and conviction tortured us equally. One moment we behaved badly and said hurtful things to one another, the other we were overcome by desire, stealing furtive rendezvous of hot sex. Furtive so not to confuse our boys, but it was we that were confused by it. Through the mess of it all, we kept returning to the shared idea that we wanted to remain committed to care for and support each other, a promise that wasn't always upheld.

Throughout the two-hour workshop taught by a social worker and pediatric psychologist, there were moments I got emotional. Everything felt so surreal, sitting there next to Dan, which felt comforting, yet we were bombarded by the do's and don'ts of broken families. I couldn't bring myself to take notes or even pay much attention. Sensing my discomfort, Dan reached over and took my hand, and as the warmth of his large, bear paw enveloped mine, my heart rate slowed, and the tightness in my throat loosened. He squeezed my hand gently. *This must all be a mistake. We are not going to go through with this; how can we?* I thought. I pulled my hand away to blow my nose, and Dan shifted in his seat and leaned in toward me, placing his hand on my thigh and knee, patting gently. His touch was the most natural thing, after twenty-five years together, yet in the time of our divorce it was also confusing and hurtful, as if his fingers were coated in coarse salt that seeped into my open, emotional wounds.

When the meeting ended, he drove me home in his truck, and pulled up outside my front door, just ten houses down from "his" house, that used to be *ours*. He didn't turn the engine off and seemed in a hurry to get going.

"Don't you think we should talk about that whole thing?" I asked. "I don't think I absorbed very much, but we have these brochures and hand-outs to look at."

After a few seconds of silence, I filled the deafening white space by quickly adding, "The boys are all set upstairs; they are making dinner and will be doing homework. We can go to Café Tisanes, just around the corner?" I looked over at him hoping he'd just park the truck and say what I wanted to hear. What I was so intensely hoping he'd say, which wasn't what I heard.

"I can't," he said instead. "I have plans."

"Plans now, at 5:30?" I think I said, staring at him, trying to force him to look me in the eyes. He was quiet and avoided my gaze. "Plans to do what?" I pressed.

"I'm going to an early movie and then dinner," he began.

"Oh?" I said, sounding more cynical than I meant.

"With Celia," he admitted.

I knew he was dating her, but a dagger slammed into my heart. In the flash of an instant, I lost my cool.

"What's with the handholding and squeezing my leg, then?" I screamed. "Does that shit not mean anything to you, and do you think I'm just a cold fish? Jesus Christ, Dan!"

I ripped opened the car door, hopped out onto the grassy patch between the sidewalk and the curb, and slammed the door shut. "Go fuck yourself!" I mumbled as I trampled toward my condo building entrance.

As soon as I got into the lobby, I regretted my strong reaction. I still had feelings for him that at times overwhelmed and confused me. But most of all, I missed *us*. His hand around mine during the divorcing parents' meeting reminded me of his typically generous spirit and re-kindled my often-played fantasy that we'd eventually get back together.

In the earlier days of our couplehood, I used to joke about how differently Dan and I would fight. He wanted to sit close, entwined even, and hold hands, while I wanted to scream and run away. This was an exaggeration, I used to say, but the day of the divorcing parents meeting, I was reminded, again, that it really wasn't. Instead, it was an accurate image of our different coping mechanisms in moments of emotional stress.

A calloused writer's bump once rode on my right middle finger, in the spot where the pen rested, lodged between my thumb and index finger. From the days before computers, when I wrote journals, letters, homework, and papers for school and university classes (and all those little blue books during exams!) with a cramped right hand, only a pale dimple remains, a tiny, cellular memorial to the era of the manual labor of writers/writing.

Today my fingers run across the keyboard of my sleek and precious iMac. The pillowy parts of my palms rest on ergonomic half-moon silicone support pillows. When typing, my fingers often become cold in the winter, like today. I never learned touch-typing, like my mom who was a secretary in her early professional life. I pause and stop and go, but the words still make it to the page on the screen in their own due time.

Sometimes I catch my hands in movements that I am not consciously planning, movements that I recognize. My dad had a certain way of reaching over toward me in the passenger seat of his car when he was driving. He would squeeze and pat my knee, *I'm happy you're here with me, I love you*, without uttering the words. I replicate this motion when I have one of my sons in the car, and every time I do, it's as if my dad is there with us. Is that what they mean by eternal life? Or "May his memory be for a blessing" as Jews say about someone who has died.

My dad's hand movements are also with me and have become mine when I peel carrots, yes, only carrots, and not potatoes. I'm standing over the sink or cutting board and hold the carrot lengthwise in my left hand, thin part pointing toward me, and rotate it slowly and mechanically to the left using the fingers of the same hand, while I run the peeler along its orange sides with long and efficient movements with my right hand. Quietly like this, my dad and I collaborate in the kitchen even many years after he is gone. I notice my hands in action and smile. He's here, now, with me, in my body's muscle memory.

Occasionally, if I am edgy or trying on clothes in the dressing room of a store, I do this jiggly thing with my fingers, as if playing quickly on the keys of a piano, but in the air, my hand hanging alongside my body. It's the most curious thing, a kind of a tic, and it's exactly what I have observed my mother do, when she seems impatient, maybe waiting for me to get ready or to give her something she is anticipating. Fortunately, now that she is in her eighties, she's more patient and so I think there's hope that this inherited finger jiggling of mine might taper off in time, too. I guess, though, that when the time comes, and my mom is no longer with us ("She should live to a-hundred-and-twenty!" as the Jewish saying goes), I might feel differently. I imagine then, that when I notice myself doing the jiggly thing with my hand, I'll smile and feel my mom right there with me, in the moment, in my hands.

Knees

Don't let your sorrow come higher than your knees.
Proverb

I've landed on my knees a few times as an adult. In the last twenty years, it's mostly in my yoga practice that I find myself on my knees, in gentle and carefully choreographed poses where I am pretty much in control of the amount of pressure I am willing to put on them. There, I'm kind to these largest and most complex joints in the body, and I prop them on an extra layer of yoga mat or blanket, to make the kneecaps more comfortable under the weight of my mature body.

My height and long legs have also put me in situations where my knees end up with the largest share of the burden. On board airplanes, for example, they often hit the back of the seat in front of me even before the person seated there reclines the seatback for their comfortable snooze, while I try to be creative in my leg-posture to avoid cramping and getting stuck. When I attend plays, shows, or concerts, especially in older theaters, I usually must squeeze my knees in place and squirm when the person in front of me leans back or worse, looks around to see what's causing the uncomfortable sensation of a pair of hard baseballs pressed against their back. I smile apologetically and try to make myself shrink.

Today a small, dark scar on my left kneecap is pain free and barely visible to the naked eye. Greyish black, as if a shadow hovers under its surface, the kidney-bean-shaped lump is raised from the lower part of my left knee cap. The scar harbors what must be some fossilized version of all the dirt once lodged under the skin-flap when I fell off my bike, at eight or nine years old. For years the scar—which has become a mere pale outline of its former self—was tender and puffy and pink, and to the younger me it seemed huge and ugly and bothersome.

The day of the spill, the wheels of my bike skidded on the gravel driveway in the courtyard of our apartment building, and I landed hard on my left side. Tiny pebbles and sand stuck under the flap of skin that hung open, like a screen door with broken hinges. My dad was home, heard my cries and whisked me up to our apartment where he put me on the edge of the kitchen sink, and rinsed my knee under lukewarm water while I whimpered and whined, snot mixing with tears.

"It's just going to sting for a while, but it's the best way to get the sand out of it," he probably said as the harsh, fresh water flushed my exposed nerves and raw tissue, trying my best to be his brave girl.

This felt very different than whenever we were on our boat and I would get a cut or a scratch, and dad would always say salt water was excellent for cleaning and healing; that the best thing would be to jump right in the ocean, which we often did. The salty water was more natural, maybe even comforting, as if it were healing tears flowing over my little compromised skin openings.

Knee protectors made out of newspaper? They were the lamest thing I'd ever seen. I'm almost sixteen and my dad is standing in front of me and my brand-new Honda moped, paper in hand. His red Dunhill cigarette lodged to one side between his lips, smoke seeping upwards past his eyes, he folds part of the weekend edition of the Norwegian newspaper *VG* into neat thirds. He is wearing jeans and a light-blue jean shirt with the sleeves rolled up, revealing his hairy forearms. His hair is dark with grey at the temples, and he smells like his Aqua Velva after shave that I love.

"Look here—let me show you how to stuff them into your pants and position them," he says. He glances at me to make sure I'm paying attention and holds two equally long and rectangular paper shapes about the width of my knees and the length of my shins, several layers thick. I roll my eyes and worry that our neighbors might be watching us in our gravel driveway, so close to the other townhouses.

"When I was in the army, we used newspaper as insulation in our uniforms, especially in the winter. Newspaper protects well from cold and wind," he explains.

He takes a drag of his cigarette, clutching it between his right middle finger that is missing the last digit and his index finger with a crooked tip. This accidental finger-amputation (middle finger) and unaligned re-connection (index finger) happened when a motor saw slipped while Dad was renovating our boat at its mooring a few years ago. He made a tourniquet and rowed himself to land, then drove to the ER with the fingertip in his mouth. He really is my hero, but now I just wave the smoke clouds away from between us, demonstratively, because I'm annoyed.

Then he shows me the newspaper trick by zipping down his fly, pulling open the pant-waist of his worn jeans, and cramming the creative protective wear down each leg. Nobody would say he isn't resourceful. "You should wear these, like so," he says and looks at me for approval, the fronts of his pant-legs bulging stiffly under his pale blue dungarees.

I have just bought a new moped with my hard-earned money, and my father wants to protect me, knowing fully that in this, his power is limited. So, he does what he can. Perched on my blue moped that I named Hjalmar, I zoom around the city streets of Oslo rain or shine, and in bad weather the knees are especially exposed to the cold, even if I wear long pants under my rain pants.

"I'm not planning on riding too much in the cold, Pappa," I try, but he ignores my feeble protest.

"If you do this consistently, it will protect your knees from getting arthritis." He pulls out the long, folded rectangles showing the weather, the comic strip, and the world news. I've often seen him rubbing his own knees. If my dad had any physical pains, it was either his back, from occasional herniated discs and prolapses, or his knees, from riding scooters and motorcycles during all sorts of climate in the 1950s.

"Like this?" I say, slowly stuffing the wads into my pants, still warm from being snug between his skin and pant-legs. I do this not without some guilt, since I most definitely will not follow his advice. *Really, Dad, newspapers in my pants?* At least he'll see that I tried.

"No need for anything fancy," he adds. "This works like a charm." Dad often spoke fondly of his service days and how he had met his best buddy, Anton, during this time. Their male bonding was reinforced each weekend they were on leave when they would hit the clubs and dance halls on the prowl for women. I imagine their social outings as live Tinder events, where they would catch glimpses of girls of all shapes, sizes, and styles, only to choose the one that they fancied, or that fancied them, ask her to dance or buy her a drink. In photos of my dad from the fifties, I think he looks handsome. There's something Steve McQueen-ish about him, which makes me imagine Dad in a glamorous way.

Dad was trying to prepare me for the upcoming summer when I was taking my scooter on a longer trip to my summer job at Anton's family resort. It wasn't actually a resort, but more like an old-fashioned boarding house, in the vein of the Italian *pensione*. A charming but not-too-fancy—even run down in places—family-operated hotel on a stunning piece of ocean front property a scant two-hour drive—by car—from Oslo.

The day I head south to Tjøme on my moped, the peninsula where the "Grepan *Pensjonat*" is located, the folded-up newspapers are stiff in my pants and bend funny at the knees. It takes getting used to the awkward feeling as I whizz out of Oslo and onto the highway. But soon, the exhilaration of the journey ahead and the prospect of all the freedom and mobility I'll have while I'm away all summer working, makes me grin from ear to ear under my blue helmet.

It's late June, school is just out, and I'm riding my fifty cubic capacity two-wheeler the eighty-plus miles to my summer job, a distance my dad and I estimate will take me and my scooter about three hours. Only part of the distance is highway, and the rest is one lane in each direction on curvy, secondary roads. I don't think it's legal to drive a scooter on the major roads, but since my parents didn't prevent me from doing it, I imagine it must be okay. I don't bother checking the rules myself. I'm wearing my helmet and figure I'll go easy and pull over along the way at gas stations and roadside snack-shacks for breaks. Cars and trucks plow by at sixty-to-seventy-miles per hour, while I only go as fast as thirty-to-thirty-five, maybe thirty-eight miles per hour if I push it, turning the accelerator handle all the way.

In hindsight, I'm puzzled my parents let me drive my puny moped on the highway, and wonder if I argued my way to it, or if they were just that relaxed? Huge eighteen-wheelers rumble past me, spitting gravel and soot my way. My hands feel numb and jittery from the vibrations of the moped handles as the little engine is pushed to max capacity, which is still too slow for the highway, and I have to take several pauses to shake them out.

My dad drives to the resort with all my stuff, his Citroen station wagon filled with my suitcase, tape player, bicycle, and several knickknacks that I will use to decorate my room-for-the-summer. The maid's lodging quarter is in a long and narrow side building where most doors open to storage spaces for linens and sheets and various retired hotel furnishings. Among the things I've brought to make my summer abode more homey are two posters—one of A-Ha, the Norwegian pop group, the other a reproduction of the French Tournée Du Chat Noir print from the 1896—a photo of my family, a wall calendar with pictures of wild horses galloping through fields (to write down my work schedule and my off days), an analog alarm clock, the round kind with a big face and four legs and two bells on top that needs to be wound once a day, and a sleeping bag for friends who might come visit me during my six-week stint.

When I finally roll down the driveway of the *pensione*, I'm exhausted and nauseous from the three-hour-long high-pitch of the little engine that could. I turn it off, put down the kickstand, and inhale the salty air, relieved to have arrived at my summer domicile safely. Seagulls squawk and float high above as I take in the familiar view of the wild rose bushes that cascade over loosely arranged boulders, outlining the edge of the pensione lawn before the small, rocky beach, right in front of the main building. Ahead, the ocean and the wide, open horizon. Somewhere beyond the horizon due south is Denmark.

That summer, my second year working at Grepan when I am about to turn sixteen, my moped makes being on the island much easier, and on my days off I zip off to places that in the past I would either walk, bike, or take the bus to reach. I relish this new level of independence. During my workdays, I am often on my hands and knees cleaning, or sitting in the afternoon sun on the kitchen stoop with a big bucket between my knees, peeling enough potatoes to feed around sixty guests their dinner.

The newspaper knee-protectors end up in the trash, not to be seen or used again, but I will always know from then onward that newspaper is a good source of insulation. And that my knees have this unique connection to fond and funny memories of my dear pappa.

·

When I pause today and notice the ongoing tenderness of my injured right knee, I'm amazed how it vividly brings back the day it got hurt, over a decade ago: the excitement, the chaos, the sounds, the embarrassment, the thrills, the disappointments.

My middle son Gabi was a senior in high school and the captain of the Hall basketball team, the Warriors, and this was their final game of the season. Playing against them was their arch-nemesis, Conard, the *other* high school team in town, the one from the *other* side of the tracks, with tougher kids and a more aggressive and often better team. Games between the two schools were tense, and students and parents in the audience were urged to behave, to not yell obscenities, and to stay in their seats.

In the fourth quarter with seconds left, the score was 41-42 with Hall down one point. If the atomic-level tension in the gym could be measured with a Richter's scale (impossible, but let's go with it), it would have been off the charts. I felt the vibrations in the metal bleachers and game sounds bouncing off the walls, as if the whole place was about to explode. Parents and students alike hollered and moaned and gasped each time there was an attempt at a basket, or a steal, or a foul, or a time-out was called. Gabi was having a great game; he was on fire. I was sweating profusely from the last few minutes' excitement as the clock ticked and the buzzer seemed to run amok with time-outs that only prolonged and heightened the suspense. It was as exhilarating as it was agonizing. The Warriors had not had a great season, nor had Gabi, and this last victory would mean the world to him, to the team.

The final moment of the game arrives, mercilessly. Three seconds left and the other team loses possession of the ball. The only way to victory for us now, is if our team makes a basket, and fast. I hold my breath. It's a collective breath-holding moment. Next is one of those rare moments when all the blood, sweat and tears (ok, and volunteer hours and driving to and from practice and games, and tournaments, and parent-coach meetings and washing sopping wet, stinky gear, and spending way too much money on just the right basketball shoes ...) are finally redeemed. What is about to happen is so big that the next day, somebody will send me a video recording from their iPhone with these precious seconds, documenting the scene. I can't say how many times I've clicked on the little play icon on the clip, which is saved right on my desktop. "Gabi's winning basket" is all of seven seconds long, and if it were an old-fashioned tape, it would have been worn thin by now from repeated wear.

What do my knees have to do with this, you are probably wondering?

When I start the brief film on my computer screen, I immediately see Gabi close to the basket with the number 25 on his back, his hands are ready and up, his teammate passing him the ball, and Gabi approaching the basket in a 1-2-3 step jump. Just as the kid recording the scene screams "Yes, Gabi!" Gabi slams it in, and the gym erupts into a massive blur of storming, flailing limbs, screams and cheers. The last three seconds of the video are completely blurry and choppy since the person holding the camera is part of this eruption, and like me, on the other side of the gym, instinctively runs toward the gym floor, while shouting hysterically.

Enter stage left: the knee memory: In my haste off the bleachers to run to Gabi, who was doing a victory dance-run on the court, I lost my footing and torpedoed toward the floor at a grotesque speed. I landed hard, and not on my feet. I had wanted to jump on and embrace my son, but instead, the tip of one of my cowboy boots must have caught the ribbed surface of the bleacher steps, causing my plummet, landing me on my knees.

In classic, stoic Nina form, I swiftly tried to pick myself up from the floor, downplaying the agony in my knees and rolling my eyes at my own clumsiness through a forced smile—*it's okay, I got this, people!* There I was sprawled on all fours on the high-gloss polyurethane floor in front of a gym filled with raucous spectators, players, journalists, schoolteachers, and just about everybody else in town. My kneecaps felt like they had been crushed, and when I tried to get up, acting as if my tumble was no big deal, they gave in under me in agony.

In that moment, I was one of those hopeless sports-parents overcome by excitement for her kid's accomplishment whose lack of common sense and impulse control is embarrassing for everyone. I eventually managed to hobble toward my jubilant son.

But once I reached the court, it was mayhem, and I wasn't even able to find Gabi. He had already zipped like lightning to the other end, where he anticipated high-fives and sweaty, exhilarated hugs and celebratory pile-ons by his team-mates, friends, and coaches. Instead, as he recounted later, he didn't know where everybody had gone, as he found himself alone and confused on one end of the court. He soon saw what was going on at the opposite end: fighting had erupted between players and fans, and the Hall and Conard kids had ended up in a cesspool of insults and fistfights. They disagreed about the accuracy of the buzzer.

School security, coaches, and teachers managed to break up the fighting, and the entire gym was evacuated. Embarrassment and shock hung heavy in the air as everyone waited outside to see what those in charge decided to do, and eventually, we were called back into the gym. To solve the disagreement, they added one second to the game, Conard missed a half-court shot, and Hall was declared the winner.

I limped home that night and could not believe that my boychik's moment in the sun had been overshadowed by such mayhem. He was happy about the win, but bummed by the drama, the outing, the finger-pointing, and investigations that ensued. A couple of the players on his team that he was supposed to have led to a glorious victory were not able to attend senior prom because of their behavior. In the news that evening and the following days it was not the winning basket and the excitement of the close game that was reported, but instead photos and video clips of the brawl and name-calling, accompanied by questions as to how it all happened.

Over the weekend that followed, a journalist from the *Hartford Courant* reached out to Gabi. He had noticed how the fracas had undermined the spirit of the sport and the extraordinary accomplishment of the winning team, and of course, of the team captain's final play that brought home the trophy. The article ran the next day, and seeing Gabi's face light up made me forget about my aching and sore knees for a good while.

However, today, many years later, I am still paying for my accidental kneeling with occasional soreness that makes me limp. I'll jump up from my writing and suddenly a shooting pain in the knee has me moaning in pain. Limping on, I groan and realize I'm essentially damaged goods, but that the detailed memory that springs from my knee is a precious treasure, after all.

When I first met Dan, everything about him made me weak in the knees. I was a nineteen-year-old au pair, about to turn twenty, in the early summer of 1985, and as much as he found my bikini-clad athletic figure, blond mane, and unreserved personality appealing (during a game of pool volleyball at the family resort where he worked and I was a guest with my host family), his dark, tanned skin, black curly hair, and gregarious demeanor caught my eye and made my insides giddy. He wore a bright pink shirt with his nickname "D-Man" embroidered above the chest pocket, and a lavender plastic whistle around his neck that he used while refereeing the game from the sideline of the pool. The things imagined by the pool that Memorial Day weekend quickly materialized into a hefty two-way flirt on day one, which turned into palpable desire by the campfire on day two, which was put into action in the early morning hours of day three in what could have easily remained a one-night stand without consequences. But instead, this tryst turned into … us. We were madly smitten with one-another, and I didn't know it then, but my life was about to take a 180-degree *volte-face*.

"Nina, the phone is for you!" called my host dad, Hank. My host family and I had left the resort, which was really a glorified campground, on a Monday afternoon, and Tuesday evening, Dan called.

"It's the guy from Strawberry Park with the pink shirt and the lavender whistle!" conservative, Korean-war-veteran Hank announced, not without some hilarity. He had questioned the young activity-director's masculinity, based on his color choices and accessories. And wasn't he just a little too jolly? It wasn't just butterflies in my belly I felt when I picked up the receiver, which hung, mustard yellow, from a six-foot-long cord off the wall-mounted phone in my host family's kitchen. That wobbly feeling in my knees came back. Ah, the delightful bodily sensations of *amore*.

.

Twenty-five years later, in 2010, twenty-two years into our marriage, I fell to my knees next to Dan in a moment of utter despair. Until then, I had never really understood what it meant when I read or heard about someone who'd "fallen to their knees" as an involuntary, emotional response. I'd conjure up images of an anemic, medieval lady who'd swoon at the sight or sound of misfortune, or distant cultures where people show grief in what stoic Norwegians—like my parents—considered greatly exaggerated ways. It was unfamiliar to me that an emotional impact could be so great that it caused your knees to buckle under you; that such a loss of physical control in a conscious moment was possible when your body was completely, seemingly, in order. How naïve I was about the power of emotional shock and trauma in and to our bodies.

In my Scandinavian, Protestant culture and family, I rarely, if ever, saw any grown-ups cry or openly express emotions like anger, rage, fear, sadness, or even frustration with much sound or gesticulations. When I was young and lived with my parents, they looked at the news in disbelief over how "dramatic" people in far-away cultures showed their grief in public; as if grief should be controlled or be a private matter in the face of war, natural disasters, violence, and loss. As a result of this early acculturation, I often cringe and easily slip into either fight-or-flight mode or feel paralyzed when someone around me has emotional reactions or gets excited or brash. The irony is that my family and friends see *me* as dramatic and loud. The glaring relativity of these points of view intrigues me, and also explains why I chose the family I did.

When my three boys were in middle and high school, Dan and I had come to loathe one another in mostly passive-aggressive ways, living parallel lives in quiet resentment, where (my) looks killed and (his) indifference wounded. Our marriage was clearly in full-blown crisis. Something had to happen, that we both knew.

Each one of us craved validation in our own ways—to be seen and heard, understood and appreciated, and somehow, we had stopped being each other's cheerleader and team-player. Numb in our own ways, we slipped away from one another. I sought out therapy, and he sought out other relationships. We also both worked out ferociously (hello mid-life crisis!)—Dan achieving various advanced grades of black belts in Brazilian Jiu Jitsu, and I, exhibiting muscular definitions on my arms and belly from power yoga and working with a personal trainer at the gym. We were in the best physical shapes we had been in our adult lives and strutted around looking svelte and content on the outside, but I, at least, felt hollow and hurting on the inside. I'm guessing Dan's Adonis-like physique and newly grown soul-patch were but outward symbols of, or diversions from, his own malaise.

Eventually I too, found the affection and attention I craved from him elsewhere, and had an affair. But I still begged for Dan to consider couple's therapy and only temporary separation, and as I obsessed about an amorous, happy ending reunion—a new beginning—I imagined, even expected, we'd treat our withering marriage the way we'd so cleverly approached the once glorious wisteria in our garden.

The climbing shrub had been long-established at the base of the raised terrace in the back of our 1914 Georgian brick house when we bought it in 1998, and we were told the plant used to give stunning clusters of light purple and fragrant blossoms. They'd hang heavy from the vines clinging to the wrought iron railing surrounding the patio, the former owner told us. But we never saw any flowers, so I researched solutions and found that one way to revive the once-blooming shrub was by using a sharp shovel to cut the roots close to the trunk, which would shock it to release its natural fight-response to the threat to its existence, causing it to flower again.

This violent, existential threat to the plant would push it to naturally summon all its energy jolting it into survival mode, and this, I thought, sounded like exactly what Dan and I were going through and what we needed. We weren't thriving anymore, and this was our blow, our shock. Our carefully nurtured roots and future as a thriving couple and little clan were threatened; we'd surely know how to rally, ensuring the future promise of our (my?) preciously earned Jewish family and our couplehood. We would bloom again; I was convinced of it.

It's early in the morning on a late winter/early spring weekday, and the boys have just been picked up for school by our car-pool. Since I didn't have to drive that morning, I'm still wearing my cozy, fleece bathrobe and felted Norwegian wool slippers. I sip my coffee in the kitchen, picking up the debris from breakfast and the hurried packing of backpacks, gym bags, and snack-packs. Our kitchen is usually a happy place with sunny yellow walls, bright-blue painted cabinets, and lively orange flooring. It's the hub of our family and a comfortably messy space, with built-in cubbies that always seem to overflow with books, games, toys, arts and craft stuff, despite my ongoing intention to organize them. An entire wall of cork board displays the boys' drawings from various stages of life, diplomas, class photos and funny, memorable family pictures: us with goofy faces, us in carnival costumes, boys jumping in water, boys playing in piles of leaves with our dogs. The half bathroom we'd put in, tucked in the corner of the kitchen by the back door, has chores charts taped to its door with masking tape. Each column has a name on top: Tobi, Gabi, Benya, and little multicolored star stickers pressed below indicating chores completed.

I start a load of darks and marvel at how much I love the front-loading washer and dryer we have finally installed in the kitchen behind a folding door, how it has made life easier not having to go into the dank basement anymore. I run the dishwasher too. The late winter morning sun enters the windows facing the driveway to the east, revealing the natural grain of our farm table that stretches long under an oversized, framed Picasso poster in bright reds, yellows, blues, and greens. The contorted and angular women stare out from the image.

Hands busy under the kitchen sink faucet, I see the wet snouts of our two Lasha Apso doggies on the lower windowpanes of the outer kitchen door, and hear a muted version of their short, staccato yelps; their way of saying, *hey, Mamma, let us back in*! So, I do, and you'd think they hadn't seen me in years, swirling all excited at my feet as I bend down to give them each a quick ruffle with my hand.

"Such good girls! Oh yeah, who's Mamma's good, good girls?" I say in Norwegian in my "dog-direct-speech," my voice in that over-the-top cartoony pitch. They lead the way toward their bowls, and I give them each a scoop of dry food and refresh their shared water bowl. After this, they'll be taking long, delicious naps on their round, plaid beds on the floor, their routine predictable.

I hear Dan stirring upstairs in our bedroom and soon I notice the water running in the pipes, which means he's in the shower. My office is also upstairs, in a large, bright room with windows in three directions, off our bedroom. I both do and don't want to go upstairs. I do because I want to get started on completing my scholar-in-residence application to a women's studies center at a prestigious New England university, but at the same time I hesitate because it will mean I'll have to face Dan. If I try to talk to him about the mess we're in, which I won't be able to *not* do, it will likely turn into a fight. I am sad and scared about his insistence that we should get divorced, and it is as if I am constantly treading on the cracking glass surface of my emotionally explosive self. I want to confront him, again, about my wish for us to "only" separate as a preliminary first step, and I have so much more I want to tell him, ask him, probe him about. I don't have the energy to, but I feel a deep urge to pummel him, beat his chest and scream and cry and beg and lose it and invoke God and our children and our parents and our relatives and friends and my therapist and our rabbi—involve them all to make him wake up and see things from a different perspective than what I feel is his tunnel vision. To see things *my* way.

I linger a bit longer in the kitchen before I slowly start up the long staircase in the foyer. I've painted these walls a deep color of eggplant and hung Moroccan lamps in an effort to turn the space into a less formal and more bohemian one. As I approach our open bedroom door, with the small, filigree mezuzah attached to its doorframe, I can smell his vanilla cologne. I think about how the tiny parchment scroll with the Hebrew writing tucked inside the delicate silver casing is believed to protect us from the evil eye and misfortune, and I summon its powers.

Hear, O Israel, the Lord is our God, the Lord is One.

Is One. I had believed Dan and I were One since I was nineteen. One couple, one unit, one love. Now, at forty-four, as I enter our bedroom, I can sense with all the fibers of my being that our oneness has splintered into innumerable, broken pieces. Shattered.

We pass each other in the small space outside my office, which is also the entrance to his walk-in closet, but nobody says anything; our bodies avoid touching on purpose even though the passage is narrow. I sit at my desk, pretend to fiddle with my computer. Every time he walks by my office door on the way to or from the bathroom or his closet, I look up, hoping he'll look toward me, that our eyes will meet, and that we can speak the way we used to—freely, openly, generously. That he'll tell me everything will be okay, and smile at me again with that gregarious smile of his that can melt any heart. Any heart. *God, when did we laugh together last?*

"If looks could kill," he says flatly, in passing.

"Don't you think we should talk?" I ask, hoping he'll reappear in the door opening.

"Nina, it's no use. You hate me. Look at the way you are seething. I can't take it anymore. I can't take the a-fib [irregular heart palpitations] that all this stress and *you* make me have. I'm dying here," he says with a dramatic emphasis on *dyyyying*. He stands in front of my desk now, just inside the door to my office. I think he looks ugly with his soul-patch, his face puffy from a poor night's sleep and maybe one drink too many the night before. Another long day and night in the office because it's tax season.

"What the hell is that supposed to mean?" I ask, my voice louder and harsher than I want. I jump up from my chair and rush toward him, feeling a flash of heat in my face, my heart racing.

"Do you think I am the cause of your fucking a-fib, you fucking moron? It doesn't occur to you that it could be your own pathetic, mean, and horrible behavior? Don't you have a conscience?" I scream.

We are facing each other now, and the entire world with all its meanings surrounding us falls away, but the windows and shelves and books and pictures and rugs and plants and papers and pens and stapler and pencil sharpener and photo albums and file cabinet and Norwegian flag and sewing machine and office chairs and dust balls, all witness, in horror, my undoing.

"What? This is why I want a divorce!" he says, "I need to protect myself and my health. You are not good for me!"

I step closer to him and start pounding his chest with my fists and cry and plead with him to have a heart and to think about the boys and that we should be bigger and better than this, and how is it possible that we're just going to fucking fold like spineless losers after two and a half decades together? Then, suddenly, without warning and with a yank of gravitational downward force over which I have no control, my knees give out and I collapse to the floor with a wretched thump, leaving me in a heap of the ugly, pilly grey fleece of my robe, complete with snot and tears and snivels. For a brief out-of-body moment, lasting perhaps a millisecond, I behold this sad spectacle that is me on the floor at Dan's feet, and I am shocked, unable to fully recognize the shape and sound of *that*.

Dan helps me up and may be trying to comfort me. I am tapped of all energy; spent like an old, wet, torn rag that's been through a spin cycle gone amok, I find myself in an alternate reality where I have never before set foot.

Dan leaves for work without much sound, and I crawl onto our king-size mattress, sprawled on the floor of our bedroom where it has been since our bedframe recently collapsed, blankets and pillows in a messy tumble. Pulling the duvet snug around me, I spend the day in bed, dozing and crying, trying to not feel how much this all hurts.

At 3 p.m., the digital, red numbers from the alarm clock on my bedside table signal I must pull myself up and out of bed because it's my turn to drive the car-pool home from school. I have to face the kids, but I don't have the willpower to get dressed. I put on my soft, blanket wool coat and twirl a long shawl around my neck, camouflaging my pajamas. I drive to school in a stupefied state, too slowly for traffic safety; I wear sunglasses, staring vacantly into the road ahead. My felt slippers are hidden in the dark under the steering wheel, and I wonder if I should push the pedal all the way down and aim for a tree.

Vagina

I was thirteen in the winter of 1979, and all I wanted was a paper-route and my period. Although I became more confident in my own body and self-awareness once I landed the paper-route—by lying about my age (I was supposed to be fourteen)—there was still one critical thing missing in my life: the thing that turned me from girl to woman. Winter turned to spring, and my warm, heavy coat and boots were traded in for a lighter jacket or sweater, and finally, sneakers, the ultimate redemption from the burden of the cold season. By now, many of the girls in my class were both more developed than I was and had begun to menstruate. It was something everyone whispered about, who had and had not gotten it was a hot topic both in and out of school, and it seemed to me that if you had it, you were part of an inner circle that the other girls who lagged envied. Sometimes, there was quite a bit of commotion surrounding the girl whose new status as a woman became known, and it was never clear to me if the tears and drama were fabricated for attention or if the distress was real. I didn't like the idea of all that attention, so as much as I wanted my period, I decided that when my turn came, I was not going tell anyone.

My mother never talked to me about what to expect, nor did she show me any feminine products or tell me how to use them. The responsibility of teaching human development and sexuality was relegated to the schools, and all I recall is *one* single "health" class taught by our teacher, the older and gentle Mr. Leinås. He had longer hair than most adults I knew, and it was grey and neatly tended. He carried a long comb in the breast pocket of his dress shirt, and several times a day he'd fish it out and give his mane three smooth runs from front to back. We'd giggle when he adjusted his dentures, but secretively I was fond of him because he complimented my drawings and taught me how to draw a straight line without using a ruler. To teach us about *human* sexuality, we watched an 8mm film about the life cycle of *frogs*, called "Peter the Frog Becomes a Father." We giggled some more and were not better prepared for any matter relating to the nature of human reproduction, but we'd remember Peter the Frog, his mating on the side of a pond and his funny looking tadpole offspring, forever.

As the spring progressed and I still did not notice anything that alerted me to the fact that I had gotten my period, I worried it would occur while I delivered the papers on my after-school route. I moved around with trepidation, although I had no idea in what way this would look or feel.

As always, I raced up the stairs in each apartment building with a stack of fresh ink-smelling papers draped over my left arm, and I tossed a copy on each doormat in front of the apartment door of the subscribing households. First floor:

Andersen on the right, Karlsen on the left; second floor: Krefting on the right, Schou on the left; third floor, nothing on the right, Berg on the left; fourth floor: Madsen on the right, Wiig on the left. Down the stairs was easy, and in a whirlwind I skipped two, sometimes three steps at a time, now empty handed, barely holding onto the banister. I often leapt over the last four steps, landing with a loud thump on the soles of my flat feet, protected by the soles of winter boots or rubber sneakers. On the ground floor of each building, I swung the front door open to find my cart with the remaining stacks of papers, pulled it by the handle to the next front door just a few meters on, and dropped the wheeled cart down again.

I was standing by my cart, checking the subscription book to see how many papers I needed for the next building when I noticed a wet sensation in my panties. *Strange. It's not like I have to pee.* Although I was a pro at holding in my pee much longer than was probably healthy, I knew what it felt like to pee in my pants. *So, what is this? Could it be …?* I picked up a new pile of papers and walked slowly into the next building, with each step trying to notice if it was getting wetter. I walked up to the fourth floor with unease, dropped a paper by each door, my mind elsewhere. I was focused on being able to tell if anything was going on between my legs, and thought about what I should do if it was blood? Knutsen, Ilseng, Bjerke, Sand, Olsen, nothing, Sturlason, nothing. Back down the stairs, but no jumping or running now. I was only halfway through my route, and there was no bathroom I could use other than those inside each apartment. *Should I knock on Mrs. Bjerke's door, the woman who had given me a pear not long ago?*

Will it be awkward? What will I say? It felt too intimate.

My mom's hairdresser was across the street, and I decided to ask if I could use their bathroom. The smock-clad hairdressers stood behind black swivel chairs with customers facing a row of mirrors, and they all greeted me with smiles and told me how much I looked like my mother. In the bathroom, I pulled down my briefs—red, polyester, stretchy granny panties—and sure enough, there was a dark stain that glistened brownish in the harsh bathroom light. With a sense of relief confused with shame and exhilaration, I pulled out a long strand of toilet paper and lined the crotch of the underwear. If this was it, I didn't know what all the fuss was about.

When I came home after I finished my paper-route, my mom was not yet home from work. I took off the soiled panties and folded them neatly and left them on top of my dresser behind a picture, perhaps hiding them as much as leaving them for her to discover. The small, decorative bumble bee patch on the front of my briefs seemed so childish now, and the patch was loose around the edges from wear and wash. Looking for a clean pair of undies, I realized for the first time that I wanted underwear more fit for the young woman I had finally become. All of the ones in my drawer suddenly looked so stupid, so juvenile.

Later that evening, when my mother discovered the stained underwear, she seemed surprised as she addressed me. "Have you gotten your period, Nina?" she asked, holding them in her outstretched hands.

"I guess so," I answered, and fought back tears. She hugged me, assured me it was the most natural thing in the world, and that she would buy pads for me. Through tears I said that I'd like some new underwear as well, and she assured me that the next time she travelled to London on business, which she did frequently, she'd go to Marks and Spencer and get me some pretty, new, cotton ones. This brief but tender moment, and the motherly promise of new, grown-up undies, made me feel special.

Finally, I was a woman.

.

Thankfully, my vagina and I have never been the victims of non-consensual penetration, which is something I realize is a blessing, especially since in today's revelatory culture rape stories and the #MeToo movement remind us that non-consensual sex is and has always been rampant.

The first time I had intercourse, I was seventeen and the guy—a Moroccan immigrant to Norway—was in his early twenties. I know I'm not the only "first-timer" to say it was uneventful, but it may be unusual that I'm not even sure how exactly it happened. Naturally, this gap I memory makes me suspicious of what actually took place.

My friend Diedra and I called him Frenchie because he spoke French with me, and I thought that was romantic (and at the time I had no awareness that the reason he spoke French was because his people and all of North Africa had been colonized by France). He was tall and lean and wore a French beret over his black locks, and, get this, a one-piece jean jumpsuit. It was the early 1980s after all, and he was into the fashion of the day. He had a sweet smile, was super charming and polite, and kind of floated around on his long legs and gentle demeanor. It happened at Diedra's house, one weekend when her mom and siblings were out of town, and we had the house to ourselves. I envision dim lights in their finished basement, where Diedra's room was located as well as a family room and a large, full bathroom. These quarters constituted the location of our forgettable encounter.

It was neither a painful nor a pleasurable experience; it just happened. It was more of a desired accomplishment than anything else. It did mark the beginning of my sexually active life, so in that, it is and was a unique moment in time.

·

It's possible that I know my vagina better than most other women know theirs, and it's because for several years I observed a Jewish custom called *taharat ha-mishpacha*, or, laws of family purity. This ancient tradition is one of the three pillars of the Jewish religious practice, which includes the observance of the Sabbath, adherence to kosher dietary laws, as well as abstaining from all forms of intimate relations during the time of menstruation.

As a Jew by choice, I felt it was important for me to practice these rituals because the more Jewish religious laws and traditions I took on in my daily life, the stronger I felt anchored in my new Jewish identity. It was not the same for me as for Dan, who was Jewish born. He could eat bacon and go shopping all day on Saturday, the Sabbath, and it would never compromise his Jewish identity or sense of cultural belonging. Rituals such as lighting Sabbath candles every Friday night, taking care never to use any dairy products when I prepared meals with meat in them, and abstaining from intimate relations —any sex at all, even touching—until my once-a-month immersion in a ritual bath that deemed me "kosher" again, were some of the cornerstones of my evolving Jewish identity.

The customary laws surrounding the practice of family purity do not just forbid sexual relations during the typical five to seven days of actual menstrual flow but extend another seven "clean" days after the bleeding and spotting ends. Of course, there are some very good reasons why this custom has remained such a pivotal part of Jewish life and survival: not only does the time of abstinence typically end at the time of the month when the woman is the most likely to conceive (and by then both husband and wife are eager to re-unite), but it's believed that when couples develop means of communication and support in other ways than relying on physical intimacy, it can strengthen their marriage and partnership.

Nevertheless, my husband who had not grown up religious, was not convinced when I suggested we should incorporate this observance into our marriage. I had to coax him to go along because it did mean a radical change from the sex-when-you-feel-like-it approach we had enjoyed in the early years of our courtship and marriage. Eventually he yielded because he saw that it was important to me.

Once a month, after my period ended and the requisite counting of "seven clean days" completed without incident, I immersed in my Jewish community's *mikvah*, or ritual bath, as a ceremonial acknowledgment of spiritual and physical renewal, before resuming intimate relations with Dan. But, before I could make my appointment at the mikvah—a small, deep pool filled with rainwater, housed in an innocuous building in town—I had to check myself internally for seven days after my period had ended, to make sure there was no spotting or bleeding. Special small white cotton swatches called *bedika* cloths are used for this purpose, that the mikvah lady attendant sold from a small wicker basket in the mikvah waiting room.

The instruction, printed on a piece of paper inside the packet, was to make an internal sweep of the vagina morning and night, and to inspect the cloth under a bright light for any discoloration. I had read and heard many stories from Jewish women who discovered both vaginal and cervical irregularities this way, and that lives were saved since early intervention had been possible. So, the ritual felt meaningful not only from a Jewish observance perspective, but also from a point of view of sensibility of health and being comfortable with and understanding my body.

For seven days after I was no longer bleeding, I draped the four-by-four square inch cloth over my index finger and felt the soft walls of my vagina and the protruding uterus on top with its little dimpled opening under the tip of my probing digit. More than anything, this practice made me appreciate the elasticity of my body, as eventually three much-larger-than-average baby boys passed through this channel.

However, one month, my habit of observing this ancient Jewish tradition was put to the test. I found myself in the middle of a delicate quandary or *sheyla*, involving my vagina and menstrual cycle, a rabbi, and his kindly wife. And that's not counting my husband who was patiently waiting in the wings for the return of our satisfying sex life ("Only four more days!" I'd wink; "Just another two days!" I'd wiggle my eyebrows and flash a complicit smile), and the gentle-mannered older woman who was the mikvah attendant.

I'm in my mid-thirties and we have three young sons. Life is busy but good. I'm a stay-at-home mom who's ABD (All But Dissertation) in a PhD program in French Literature. Instead of doing research and writing about mighty philosophical and literary queries, I'm invested full-time in my Jewish family life, teeming with the Jewish customs that I have come to love and cherish. I "do" Jewish every day of the week, every

Sabbath and every holiday. I have come to incarnate a merger of two epic empires: that of the *yiddishe mama* and the *balabusta*—the ultimate Jewish homemaker who cooks not just to feed her family but also for guests most Sabbaths—and I deftly managed *yiddishkeit* full throttle as the CEO of the Lichtenstein Household.

Instead of counting the pages of dissertation chapters, I'm counting the days of my cycle. In Jewish tradition there's a lot of counting, which at times can feel obsessive. We especially count our blessings, but never our children. Counting souls is believed to invite the trouble of the *ayin harah*, or the evil eye.

My period is over, and I am tallying the seven days with no bleeding or spotting. I feel the urge at a visceral level to be intimate with my husband again, and when I shower, I close my eyes and imagine how good it will be to have his hands running over my body. Lips, hands, breasts, legs, hips and genitals tightly connected; our breath close and our union affirmed.

Two more days and I will call Judy the mikvah lady or *shomeret*, to make my appointment. After sunset on the seventh day, I'll make sure my hubby will be home with the kids as I'll scurry off in the dark (for discretion) to the non-descript white colonial on Main Street where the small pool of running spring waters will symbolically render me "clean," again, for marital relations. Before I immerse in the mikvah, I plan to spend a good hour in one of the building's two full bathrooms, each with a door that opens to the small pool area. In the bathroom that is equipped with everything I need from Q-Tips to nail-polish remover, hair dryer and dental floss, I will soak in a warm bath, remove my make-up, clean and cut my toe and finger nails, brush and floss my teeth, and comb my long, often knotted hair, making sure the teeth of the comb run smooth so that there are no obstacles preventing the water of the mikvah to reach and surround all parts of me, even every strand of hair.

Once I am ready, I will ring a small buzzer mounted by the door in the bathroom, alerting the attendant to meet me poolside. Before I descend the seven steps[1] into the living waters, as they are often called, she will examine me, front and back, gently brushing her warm hands over my body to make sure no loose hairs remain and checking in between my fingers and toes for any hidden specks of lint so that nothing will come between the water and me.

One-two-three-four-five-six-seven; I'll step down into the water which is warm and welcoming, the turquoise and beige tiled walls of the pool forming a rectangular space not much larger than six feet by six feet. Once I stand on the bottom, the water will reach to just above my breasts. I've done it so many times I have lost count, yet each time I stand here feels like the first; I feel vulnerable but safe, spiritually lifted, yet grounded in the practical steps of the ritual. I'll take an inhale and dunk under, bending my knees, simultaneously making sure my feet lift from the bottom of the pool and my head and hair are fully immersed. For a second or two, nothing touches me but the water in the mikvah; I am an embryo floating protected in amniotic fluid, ready to emerge into a new beginning. When I stand back up, Judy will hand me a small washcloth that I use to cover my head—married women traditionally cover their head—and I'll keep my hands crossed over my

---

1 According to the Torah, God created the world in six days, but made it complete with the Sabbath, the seventh day. The number seven suggests wholeness and represents the creative process, and thus the seven steps leading into the mikvah.

breasts, for modesty.

"Blessed are You, Adonai, Ruler of the Universe, who has sanctified us with mitzvot and commanded us concerning immersion," I'll recite the blessing in Hebrew with my eyes closed. Then I'll immerse two more times.

"Kosher!" Judy will exclaim. "Take your time to get out, sweetheart," she'll add, knowing many women relish a few moments of quiet time to meditate or simply just be.

But wait a minute! Later that day, the fifth day of the seven clean days that I am counting, I notice a couple small brown specks, the size of lentils, in my panties. *Oh shit, say it isn't so.* I'm spotting. I check myself internally with the thin, delicate bedikat cloths again to see if maybe it was just a fluke. But there is more. *Oy.* Oy is right. I call up the mikvah lady to ask her advice. She tells me to call the wife of the supervising rabbi, the *rebbitzen*, who will act as an intermediary so as to ensure anonymity between me and her husband, who is the local authority on the many minutiae of Jewish law as it pertains to the mikvah.

I hear her young children's voices in the background when she tells me that in order for her husband to make the appropriate ruling, he needs to see the spots. A wave of confusion mixed with mortification washes over me. I am asked to place the "evidence" in a zip lock bag in an envelope and drop it off after dark (again, for discretion) in their mailbox at their residence.

I know this rabbi and his lovely wife. Their kids are in the same school as my kids. They have dedicated their lives to helping Jews observe Jewish traditions, and they both do it with kindness and wisdom. As I listen to the rabbi's wife give me instructions, I sit in a time-worn red-velvet wing-back chair near the window in the den of our house; the door is closed. Far away I hear my children fighting and our two dogs barking. The chair seems to be levitating in the air. With me in it.

Outside the window, the birds flutter soundlessly in the overgrown rhododendron bushes whose green, leathery leaves press up against the beveled glass panes of the leaded windows. I see their small yellow beaks open as they chirp eagerly – angrily? – at each other, negotiating who will have a turn next at the birdfeeder stuck to the window with suction cups.

My fingers feel prickly and numb and there's a buzzing in my ears. To be a bird right now and fly away. My cheeks and neck flash hot and warm and I'm cold sweating. I sit slumped in the hand-me-down chair, holding the phone against my pounding ear, imagining the rabbi examining my underpants.

Later that evening, the rabbi's wife calls me back. It's late and my kids are in bed, and Dan is still at work.

"So, my husband checked …" she begins gently. I take a deep breath and feel embarrassed again.

"Unfortunately, he says you will have to start counting the seven clean days again," she continues. "From the beginning."

The prickly sensation I had noticed during our first conversation earlier in the day returns, and I am not in my body, but outside of it. Shame and indignation fill both spaces, the ghost of me and the other me, weighing me down doubly.

"You are kidding?" I say and realize how stupid that sounds the second the words tumble out of my mouth.

"I am sorry," she says. "Are you normally regular?"

"Yes, like clockwork," I say, thinking how it will be impossible to continue observing this *mitzvah* if this is how my body will behave.

"Well, hopefully, this is just a fluke," she says.

"I sure hope so," I answer. "Ok, thanks for your help. Good night."

"Okay, take care," she says. "If you have any questions, you can call me anytime," she adds.

We hang up.

I don't count the new seven days, and I don't go back to the mikvah again. But this decision also comes with regrets. The ancient monthly ritual had provided me with an important framework for my identity as well as a meaningful element in my marriage. I will come to miss my monthly pilgrimage to the white colonial on Main Street, my quiet chats with Judy, and the excitement of returning home to my husband, both desired and desirous.

In hindsight, I think what happened with the rabbi, his wife, the mikvah attendant and me that day was a small trauma, if trauma can be measured in size.

More than ten years later, when my husband and I decided to separate and I was packing to move out of our house, I discovered a forgotten packet of the little, white bedikat cloths in the bottom of a wicker box where I kept tampons and pads. I held the clear plastic baggie in my hand, a delicate drawing of a rose decorating the front. With a sigh that held the breath of generations of women, I tossed it into the trash. Then I paused for a split second, reached in and pulled the packet back out of the garbage can. I opened the lid of the wicker storage box and tucked the bedikat cloths back in with all my other feminine products. I wasn't ready to let go.

.

Today, it has been over twenty years since I stopped going

to the mikvah. I no longer have periods, so the "laws of family purity" no longer need to be observed, even if I were to get married again. After my divorce, I eventually moved away from the town and state where we had raised our three sons and where I had lived for nearly thirty years. There, I had been deeply engaged in the Jewish community which also functioned as a protective wall around my identity as a Jewish woman. Leaving the place where I had done so much fostering of cultural roots, both spiritual and relational, has been difficult yet liberating. Although I'm still a practicing Jewess by most definitions, I no longer observe Judaism in the same strict way I used to in my younger days. Happily, it does not make me feel any less Jewish. I guess the Jewishness I was not born with has embedded itself over time in the fibers of my body and in the breath of my being, but deep down I know that it took *all that* to get here.

Below is a poem about the messy and scary birth of my youngest son, Benya. Experimenting with a lyrical, flowing frame for this memory has helped me transform a complex and confusing experience into something I actually … like. It has allowed me to shape the memory, and this is empowering considering how powerless a woman can feel in the moment of birthing.

A Bloody Mess

I.

The little one, who was big,
slipped out easily after a few determined pushes;
my third child.
Jesus Christ, what a bloody mess
embarrassed that I soiled the ceiling in the birthing room.
Looking up through bloodstained glasses, the midwife pushed
back
from between my wide-open knees with an "oops!"

The man who held the scissors turned pale;
he was the father of the baby, a boy.
The cord was fat and difficult to cut,
with the warm and deep red life force pulsing through it,
out of it,
and onto the walls,
the ceiling,
the floor,
the midwife's face.

Swoosh. Here he was, outside of me,
forever, ready to take his first breath,
ready to scream at a life that could be blessed
or cursed.

And he did.

II.

Why does it still hurt? I asked.
The midwife caught the eye of the nurse
who swept the baby and the father away
and with an experienced and calm move
pushed the short round stool on wheels closer
holding a metal pan in one hand, and with the other hand,
her entire hand,
she reached inside me
and pulled out a mass of coagulated blood.

III.

When they brought my baby to me
after we were all cleaned up,
it struck me how lucky I was to be alive,
and how some of life's messiest things
bring the biggest miracles.

Back

I got my own back.
Maya Angelou

It happened in the bathroom as I turned to reach for the toilet paper. I felt something snap and knew immediately that I'd thrown out my back. The accident left me useless *and* helpless but wasn't as much an accident as an unavoidable malfunction of my thirty-six-year-old body that had carried three full-term pregnancies in little over four years.

For a few days before, I had noticed something was not right, and I moved with a cautionary edge that made me wary of lifting and bending. I was hyper attuned to any small twitch or change. This was after all a body part that had become particularly vulnerable after carrying huge babies, first in my womb, then in my arms and on my hip, often all three places simultaneously. Our way-above-average babies (read: off the chart in height and weight) inherited a combination of my own Norwegian-Viking genes, and those of my 6'4" tall Jewish husband and his Russian ancestors: the mythical Curgansky's, or the Kurgans of the Russian Steppe, known for its giants (really). The abdominal abuse of multiple pregnancies, weight gain, and subsequent lack of exercise had finally caught up with me.

For as long as I can recall, I've always been the one to give others a ride on my back. When we played "house" or "farm" during recess in school, I was never the mom or the dad. Never, of course, was I one of the kids; I was too tall, so by default I was the work horse. A head taller and much stronger than all the other classmates, boys included, my career as a service mammal began early.

As a teenager, I carried girlfriends on my back for fun, their long legs dangling heavy to my sides, and while babysitting I gave countless children a rest during hikes. Little, clambering, human monkeys enjoyed free rides up the stairs to coax them into their bedtime routines. Throughout my young-adult life, I was always able and willing to do hard, physical work, especially if it meant assisting others or earning some spending money.

Need help moving furniture? Call Nina! Have some garden-bins that should be hauled? Nina to the rescue! Stones? Firewood? Crates full of stuff? I've got it. No, no, let me!

As a wife, it was I who schlepped our three massive trash cans up our long, winding driveway to the curb every Tuesday night, and as the ultimate Jewish housewife or *balabusta* elbow deep in preparations for Passover, I dragged the huge plastic crates filled with kosher-for-Passover china, pots, pans, glasses, and silverware up the basement stairs, pregnancy be damned.

When I had my own three kids, it wasn't just their dad who was big and strong and physical; boisterous romps and wrestling matches were plentiful with both Mamma and Pappa. It was all fun and games until the day my back went out—the kind of breakdown that made an invalid of this usually invincible woman and mother of three energetic boys under the age of six.

Injured, I could do little else with the kids except kiss them and remind them to be careful when they crawled into my bed to be close to me. "Don't jump!" "No roughhousing!" "Be gentle with Mamma!" No more giving them baths, frolicking on the floor, or lifting them for those yummy belly-to-belly hugs. Even helping them dress was too difficult, as was wiping their tushies or cooking their meals. Our Norwegian *au pair*, Karoline, had just arrived from Norway the week before my collapse, and although it was a rough initiation for her—like jumping into icy water without any preparation—she didn't just float; she swam heroically, carrying our three little, big cubs on her back as if they were her own.

That day on the toilet, it was what should have been a small, inconsequential rotation that caused the lumbar discs to slip and put the debilitating pressure on nerves so significant that, trying to stand up, I collapsed to the floor with a loud cry. Dan, who had not yet left for work, came running in from the kitchen. Unable to get up by myself, he lifted me from the floor and carried me up the stairs to our bed, while I screamed like a hog going to slaughter.

I had no potent painkillers on hand, only Tylenol and Advil, neither of which touched the pain, so I writhed in it until a friend who is an ER doc was able to come to the rescue. Commuting between hospital jobs in the US and Israel, Dr. Mark used to stay on our third floor when he worked his ten-day shifts in the States. Thankfully, he was local and able to come to the rescue, an hour or so later.

"Tell him I need something strong to kill this fucking pain!" I moaned as Dan was on the phone with him, explaining what had happened. "Ask him to come as soon as he can! I'm dying here!" In the relatively brief waiting period before he arrived, time was as if sadistically suspended, leaving me in some evil version of purgatorial torture.

When Mark finally walked through our bedroom door, his appearance was the arrival of the Messiah—the promise of redemption-incarnate. Known as a doctor with superior bedside manners, he looked into my eyes with empathic concern; he listened intently and agreed that I needed something stronger to help with the pain. I swallowed the pills he gave me, closed my eyes, and prayed they would work fast.

I will never forget the relief as the meds began to work some twenty minutes after I inhaled them; that warm, numbing, and floaty sensation that I first noticed as tiny, giddy, bubbles making their way through each limb toward my core as if they were alive and rushing to a party, gathering a gentle intensity as the minutes passed, until finally, all the agony in my lower back evaporated—or was it I who evaporated?— until I didn't really care about anything, except the blessed absence of pain. Enveloped in in this artificial bliss, resting on a cloud of mercy, my body and mind levitated far away from any possible calamity, every square inch of me sinking heavy and limp into the mattress.

This salvation was what my body quickly learned to crave. My early redemptive meetings with the now infamous prescription pills Hydrocodone (AKA hydros, lorries, Watsons, 357s), Percocet (AKA Percs), and OxyContin (AKA kickers, blues, hillbilly heroin), meant to be for temporary use until I healed, turned out to be the beginning of my brush with opioid addiction.

In the early days of the injury, when I had to use the bathroom, I made sure I was good and drugged up before venturing out of my horizontal and pillow-propped position in bed. I would slowly inch my way down onto a blanket that my husband positioned on the floor next to our bed, carefully situating myself on all fours so he could pull the blanket with me on it without me losing my balance, to the adjoining bathroom.

I felt the hard threshold under my knees, as Dan slowly tugged on the blanket to get me onto the bathroom's tile floor. He hoisted me to the toilet seat; he helped me wipe. To shower, I knelt on all fours on the cold tile floor as Dan used the hand shower to try to wash me as best he could, complicated by the fact that I was unable to lift my arms or legs. Awkward in this tabletop position, I'd shake from freezing and keep my eyes closed as if to save myself from the view of my own pitiful state, the room spinning around me, while I begged in a whimper, "It's enough, Dan, it's enough. Please just dry me off."

After about one week flat on my back with the worst of the discomfort continually numbed by the "good" drugs, I worked out an effective routine of timing the next dose in order to stay ahead of the pain. I was petrified by the possible return of the monstrous agony and had yet to realize that the real monster was what I put in my body every four hours, or three and half, to be safe and avoid a lag.

Our friend Mark—who I saw as my fairy godmother—sat on the edge of my bed one morning, sipping coffee before he had to head to the hospital. We talked about the various options for my situation. "We should get you an MRI as soon as you are able to get to the radiology center," he said. I nodded, unable to see myself moving any further than to my bathroom. "When we have those results, you should make an appointment with a neurosurgeon or orthopedic surgeon, or both. We'll want to hear their opinions and recommendations."

I was already overwhelmed at the prospect of "opinions and recommendations" and just wanted it all to go away. I sighed and checked the time; still another half an hour before I could take two more pills. "Hopefully we can avoid surgery and you'll be able to begin physical therapy as soon as you can walk again," he concluded, gently patting the blanket that covered my legs. His kind eyes met mine and I felt comforted that he understood my misery.

"Make sure to drink plenty of water because the pain meds can cause constipation," Mark added.

"Um, yeah, I've noticed," I said, resigned. "The problem is, I'm afraid to drink because then I'll have to go to the bathroom. It just hurts so damn much to move." He asked if I wanted him to bring me a bedpan, and I said sure, as my former independent self, sank deeper into accepting my state of helplessness.

The TV that Dan had rigged up for me at the foot-end of our bed was muted but on, and while Mark and I chatted away, the screen suddenly showed an airplane approaching the North Tower of the World Trade Center, then crashing into it. We turned on the volume and flipped between channels to hear Katie Couric and Wolf Blitzer report with incredulity what the nation watched with them.

Seeing the towers collapse while I was cocooned in the artificially induced comfort in my bed, I felt no dread or adrenaline rush, as I am sure I would have, had I not been on such strong painkillers. During that day's endless replays of falling, fleeing, and bloody people, floating ashes, and flying debris amid wails and screams, I watched and listened, but without the visceral empathy I usually experienced when I see humans or animals suffer. While Americans realized the scope of the 9/11 devastation, and shared grief took hold of the nation, I drifted in and out of a cottony, painless place between reality and dream.

This was in 2001, several years before the opioid crisis was named, and during a time when doctors prescribed narcotic pain relievers without much restraint or warnings. Prescription opioids volumes peaked in 2011, and from 2007-2017, heroin overdose-deaths increased five-fold. We didn't know the dire statistic then, that individuals who are addicted to prescription opioids are forty times more likely to become addicted to heroin, and that heroin is both cheaper and easier to get a hold of than refills of your pain meds.

All I thought about was how to have enough of my tiny round pharma-saviors—the "lorries" and the "kickers"—on hand, so that the pain that had ambushed every neuron, muscle, and bone around my lower back would not return. If I stayed on top of it, I was able to lift my hips off the mattress enough and without too much discomfort so that Dan could push the bedpan under my butt when I had to pee.

After about ten days, when Mark returned to Israel, I managed to eke my way out of bed to a standing position. This probably meant that my body had begun its slow process of healing, but other than that I could now stand and slowly walk on an even surface, I was unable to tell because I was continually medicated. After the MRI and a consultation with an orthopedic surgeon (who offered to operate the same week) and a neurosurgeon (who advised me to let my body heal itself) I saw a physiatrist, the kind of doctor whose specialty it is to help patients manage chronic pain.

The moment when I might not have needed such strong meds but continued taking them anyway is unclear. Several weeks went by with me limping slowly down the unbearably long corridors to the physiatrist's office, where he consulted with me before I received ultrasound treatments. Although I was slowly improving and taking the pills at longer intervals during the day, I was still on them regularly, and especially before bedtime, when I upped the dose to make sure I could have a decent night's sleep, uninterrupted by the throbbing ache that still made it impossible to sleep and excruciating to turn in bed. At night, after the kids were in bed, I'd take an extra pill and wait for it to send me off to la-la-land, not caring if it made me drowsy and unable to read or talk with Dan. The longed-for and effervescent warmth spread through my body, lifting me away from everything. By day's end I craved its effect with desire, as if it were an amorous encounter with a lover I anticipated.

It had become a shady time, dictated by a profound dread of the acute agony I remembered from the early days of the accident and heralded by what were likely the obvious symptoms of addiction, at least to the doctor who managed my pain.

Life outside my opioid lined cocoon could be an unpleasant place: terror, loss, fear, Al Qaeda, national paranoia, and xenophobia. We had an Egyptian brother–in–law whom my three sons adored and who suddenly disappeared, unwilling or unable to deal with the hostility and pressure of being an Arab in the US in the wake of 9/11. Times were ugly and my altered state muffled that noise.

One sunny, early-winter day, after hobbling to the physiatrist for several weeks and after many "regular" refills, I asked him for yet another refill. But instead of scribbling the answer to my request on a script, to my horror, he suggested it might be time to cut back on the painkillers and begin phasing into non-prescription alternatives. It makes me cringe now, realizing how I essentially argued with him, probably desperate sounding, trying to assure him that I was still in enough pain to warrant the strong meds.

He was not convinced, and I was so upset at the prospect of going home with no more of the good stuff that I began to cry. He was not moved, and I felt a wave of humiliation, my cheeks flushing red, as if my pathetic travesty had been revealed. Instead, he recommended a spinal Cortisone injection, which might, if I were lucky, block any residual pain enough to enable me to continue with the physical therapy and swimming I had managed to incorporate into my rehab routine. I agreed, despite the minute but very real risk of paralysis that any injection in the spine might cause.

The following week, clad in a green disposable paper smock and hair net, I signed the consent form that the anesthesiologist handed me. Stretched out on a paper-lined examining table at my local hospital, I pushed away thoughts of the worst-case scenarios it listed (spinal headaches: not common but possible; paralysis: extremely rare, but a risk nobody wants to be liable for). I was so eager to do *anything* to prevent the return of the pain—pain that by now might have been more imaginary than real—that none of the risks mattered.

The afternoon following the Cortisone injection, the reality of my addiction reveals itself. I'm resting at home on our red sectional couch in the den, my husband brings me dinner on a tray, and the boys dart in and out of the room. I encourage them to join me on the couch for a cuddle while we watch re-runs of Sesame Street, or Arthur, or Clifford the Big Red

Dog. I have not taken any pain meds since before I went to the hospital that morning, now going on eight hours. Every minute, I anticipate the return of the throbbing discomfort that has kept me psychologically hostage for so many weeks, but that I have almost forgotten what it actually feels like. I don't allow myself to be optimistic that the injection might have been successful. I'm just relieved the procedure did not leave me paralyzed. I gently adjust my position on the couch. Does it hurt? Is the pain back? No, nothing yet. A few more hours go by, and that's when I begin to realize that the shot must be working, and that I am probably going to be pain-free for at least a month or two, while my back will continue to heal. With all the physical and other therapies that I am signed up for, perhaps by then, the worst will be over.

When the boys' bedtime rolls around, I am able to get off the couch, and still nothing hurts. I am not woozy since I have not taken any narcotics. I feel a bit naked on the inside, as if I must reacquaint myself with what it's like to move around in this body. I am almost afraid to be happy, to jinx it. For the first time in many weeks, I can put the boys to bed, help them brush their teeth, get them into their pajamas. I can even sit by their bedsides to read them each a story.

That night, I go to bed with relief. The small brown bottles of prescription meds sit on my nightstand, where I have kept them within arm's reach for the habitual refill halfway through the night. I push them aside. Finally, I can stop taking them and won't have to humiliate myself by asking my doctor for refills. I fall asleep with gratitude and full of hope.

When I wake up at 4 a.m., I change position from my left side to my right side, where I haven't slept since it all began. No pain. *This is too good to be true. I must be dreaming*, I think.

Boy, am I lucky if this really holds. I smile as I doze off, imagining the improved quality of life I can look forward to. Dan's regular breathing next to me comforts me. But soon I'm uncomfortably warm, almost feverish. And then chills. I get up for a drink of water and my stomach hurts. *Oh great, what the hell is this? Am I getting the stomach flu, now?* I go back to bed hoping it will pass, willing myself to visualize a positive outcome, picturing that perhaps I'm just reacting to the injection. Eventually, I do fall asleep, despite a sense of restlessness and worry about what the next development might be.

The following day, my head hurts, but it's mild enough to ignore. Karoline is bright and cheery at the kitchen sink, where she's swigging her customary tall glass of early-morning water. Our au pair from Norway is a slender nineteen-year-old with shoulder-length, light-brown hair in an efficient ponytail, and she moves swiftly about. Inspired by her healthy habits, I pour my own glass of water but struggle to drink it on an empty stomach. I look over at Karoline and the boys seated around the kitchen table, enjoying bowlfuls of Oat Squares and Honey Nut Cheerios, and I marvel at how they talk so naturally together—as if they have known each other for years—among chats and giggles, occasionally interrupted by brief tiffs between the boys. I observe how well she handles each of their temperaments with patience and calm authority, and I am an outsider in my own kitchen. There's a pang somewhere inside me as I watch my kids in a moment to which I've lost the key, and I'm on mute, excluded from the intimate language of our family's daily ritual.

I have missed countless mornings of this ritual since Karoline's arrival and notice she has competently figured out the ropes by herself, neither Dan nor I able to be of much help; me due to being bedridden and drugged up, him because of the crazy 24/7 work schedule of the self-employed. After breakfast, when it's time for the boys to brush their teeth before she whisks them off to nursery school and kindergarten, she stands next to our deep, stainless steel utility sink, one foot on top of an old, wooden step stool, a hand-me-down painted in the pale blue of the 1950s with faded flowers on the side. There, Karoline nimbly hoists my middle son's lanky four-year-old body up on her knee, where he balances with a big grin, one leg dangling down on each side of hers. I feel a sting at their intimacy and immediately admonish myself. This has obviously become their little routine—her way of getting our little monkey to cooperate with tooth brushing, avoiding negotiations as departure time quickly nears.

Once the boys are out of the house, I rest on the comfy red couch. In the silence of the house I slumber, the warmth of Yoffie and Shooggie next to me, one curled up at my feet, the other stretched out alongside my body. I wake when my stomach begins to cramp and head to the bathroom. As I sit on the toilet, diarrhea pouring out of me, my legs begin to shake, my knees hurt, and my muscles ache. Chills make my shoulders shudder, mixing with sweat on my forehead and chest, and unstoppable waves of the nausea from last night return, warning of an inevitable and dangerous undertow. *What is going on?* Weary and weak, I make my way back to the couch and into a fetal position, anxiously awaiting the next bout.

While I doze, I am startled by my phone ringing; it's my friend Melissa calling to check in on me. Phone in one hand, I'm back on the toilet, shaking. She is a psychiatrist with an acute and sensitive knowledge about pharmaceuticals.

"Have you stopped taking your pain meds?" she asks. "Yes," I tell her, I haven't needed any since the Cortisone shot seems to have hit the spot, and the last time I took Percocet was about thirty-six hours ago.

"Oh Nina," she says, "You are going through withdrawal." Her voice is grave as she tells me symptoms can be both painful and debilitating. It takes me a few moments to connect the dots between the severity of what she is telling me and how I must have lived with a dependency whose force I had not grasped.

"Are you serious?" I ask. All I can think is what I know about how "real" drug and alcohol addicts suffer terribly when they try to get clean. My late father—who called himself "an atypical alcoholic" since he drank daily but thought he did not behave like a drunkard—had told me all about "the shakes" or *delirium tremens* as he called it. But I never considered it to have any relevance for me.

"Didn't your doctor tell you to wean yourself?" she asks, sounding incredulous.

"No, nobody said anything about weaning. I just stopped, and now I guess my body is reacting," I reason, wondering if this is the worst of it, or if there will be more. She assures me the symptoms will eventually taper off, most likely within a day or two, and that it isn't as dangerous as it is disagreeable.

"If it gets worse, I can prescribe something to relieve the symptoms," she offers.

After we hang up, I turn on my computer and do a quick search, and sure enough, my flu-like symptoms are characteristic of Percocet and opioid withdrawal. The website also lists other, more scary indications, like shallow breathing and increased heart rate. I close the laptop and my eyes and try hard to think happy thoughts.

Days passed, my back didn't hurt me at all, and the withdrawal discomforts I had felt the first few days after I stopped taking the opioids eventually ceased. Soon, I began a more active path to recovery, and my days were filled with appointments for physical therapy, acupuncture, ultrasound treatment, and swimming, and I no longer hobbled down the doctor's office hallways.

After a long fall and winter spent in a woozy drug-induced haze, spring with its promise was finally around the corner. I relished being able to again be fully involved with my boys and all their activities. Days passed in once-familiar routines that had never before felt like such a blessing, so welcome, so comforting, so delightfully uneventful.

In the weeks and months following my recovery—even several years later—a small brown bottle with narcotic prescription meds sat in my bathroom cabinet, "in case I should have an acute back situation again," as I kept telling myself. But even if I just had a bad headache or felt a little down or funky after a shitty day, it was as if my tiny, potent friends were beckoning me from inside the bottle. A fake, callous posse calling from a place I knew I shouldn't venture into, they sounded all chill and enticing, promising a few hours of dreamy, floating respite.

Respite from what? At what cost? I ask myself, but any clear answer escapes me. Sometimes out of nowhere and feeling urgent, all I want is to crawl back inside of that softly padded tunnel of bliss again, just once more.

Brain, Mouth, and Butt

A Body Parts Conspiracy Theory

I'm burdened with what the Buddhists call
the "monkey mind"—the thoughts that swing
from limb to limb, stopping only to scratch
themselves, spit and howl.
Elizabeth Gilbert

"Nina disrupts the class," reads one faded report card from my elementary school days in Norway. Another one reminds me, "Nina leaves her desk and walks around in the classroom without permission." The pile of report cards, a testament to my early history as an impulsive disruptor, are all penned in Ms. Halstensen's neat, cursive, blue fountain pen handwriting, on old, yellowed paper that smells sweet and musty. I rummage through a file folder my mother has saved for me, holding keepsakes from my childhood. I was regularly sent out of the classroom to "stand in the hallway," as the punishment was called, which was basically a time out for the student in question to calm down and get a grip about conforming to classroom order.

As a kid, I often visited older folks in my apartment building or next door, some of them shut-ins, listening to their stories or telling them mine, while sharing a snack or a cup of tea, getting familiar with the look of their thin, wrinkled skin and their warm eyes reflecting loneliness into mine. I'd sneak furtive glances at their toothless, cavernous mouths where pink gums hid behind dry lips, helping them carry their groceries or walk their dogs. Of course, the truth is, I didn't just stir trouble as the latchkey kid I was, but yearned to be seen and heard, and with our apartment key dangling in a cotton string around my neck, every afternoon, day in and day out, our city block was my queendom to rove as I pleased.

"Freedom with responsibility," my parents and their friends called it the early seventies, assuming that even though they let us kids roam free, unattended, we'd know to make sound (enough) choices to stay out of too much trouble; if we didn't, it was healthy life-experience gained, as far as our parents were concerned. It's possible I would have preferred less freedom when I was seven, eight, and nine, and perhaps a more structured, boundary-defined routine, but the premature independence of us latchkey kids was a staple of my generation. One benefit of this developmental paradigm is that we turned into a resourceful bunch who saw the world as our oyster and were rarely intimidated by the unknown. Our parents were at work, and Oslo was a safe enough place to let kids get by on their own after school and into the evenings. I would knock on doors around mealtime to invite myself in, and I'm guessing I was probably hungry for more than food.

I've often puzzled at my fondness and attraction to older people because I have always sought out their companionship in a way my peers never seemed to do. From my early childhood years hanging out with seniors in my building and on our street, to a fondness for my parents' friends' parents, or the older guests at the inn where I worked during my teenage summers in Norway, to gravitating to older boyfriends and lovers, it has been a constant in my life. Aside from being called an old soul from early on, I suspect it has to do with the need I have always had to feel seen, and to feel special, which is a gift older people often give to younger ones, as time slows down and their lives become less hectic. They may be as thrilled about the attention, curiosity, and validation afforded them by a young'un, as I have been by what they give me; an opportunity to shine and to matter. The fact that my current life partner is twenty-seven years my senior is a testament to this penchant—or need?—of mine.

I have come to realize that my brain, mouth, and butt have been in cahoots ever since I was that young child, brewing mayhem and scheming insubordinations landing me in plenty of trouble. Why "butt" and not "legs" you might say, if my getting in trouble involved moving around too much, too often, as if driven by a force I couldn't control? Because aren't children raised to believe that to "sit still," whether in school, in church, in adult company, or at mealtime, is what makes a good girl or good boy? And we sit on our butt, don't we? Even as an adult and a writer, I think daily about one of my favorite gurus for writing advice, Anne Lamott, who chants her favorite mantra "Butt in Chair" as the path to becoming and being a writer. My butt has a mind of its own, though— always have, always will—and in this has preferred to remain independent and not glued to a chair for any substantial amount of time. (See notes above on my report-cards from elementary school.)

Thankfully, as I grew older and entered middle school and high school, I understood what it would take to charm my teachers enough so that I wouldn't get in too much trouble despite my impulsive behavior. I must have figured out how to self-censor (I assume by trial and error) to avoid being expelled from class or sent to the principal's office as often as in my early years. Thanks to attributes like my neat handwriting, and good scores on most tests and assignments, I dug myself out of the potentially damaging but typical situation of the energetic and nonconforming child being stereotyped as "difficult." It may have helped that I was a girl, since "difficult" boys never received as much benefit of the doubt and second (or third or fourth) chances.

The older I got, the more I became personable and polite, most of the time, and developed the skill to please those who might judge or punish me—a typical "self-help" solution used by resourceful kids with behavioral issues—often relating more easily to adults than to kids my own age. It felt good to be liked by the adults, finally, and the "bad girl" stigma slowly transformed into "good girl" as far as the teachers were concerned. However, for most of my middle-and high-school years, I felt like an outsider among my classmates, but accepted and embraced among adults, especially older folks, as noted earlier.

It was in middle and high school that I turned all my energy and "pleaser" urge into a productive and lucrative asset, holding down several after-school jobs keeping me busy during weekday evenings and weekends. Always on the move, I was otherwise occupied while my peers did more typical tween and teen things like getting into trouble at parties, laden with romantic dramas and intrigue, exploratory sexual encounters, and often, alcohol.

The newspaper route I landed by lying about my age was an early feat in a series of gainful employments that filled my teenage years. When I was found out—by the third or fourth paycheck—the boss at the newspaper central let it slide, not wanting to lose a conscientious papergirl. By then, I'd turn fourteen soon enough, the required minimum age for a paper route. At this same age, I already had several regular babysitting gigs and at fourteen, began cleaning the sprawling apartment of my home-economics teacher's parents, a weekly job I kept until I graduated from high school and left for America at eighteen. At sixteen I landed a twice-a-week after-school job in Oslo's only Original Levi's store, becoming solely responsible for running one of the branches on Saturdays, the only weekend day it was open, and only from 10 a.m. to 3 p.m. This was the era before malls and online stores, and before the advent of the 24/7 shopping culture.

I oozed with grown-up confidence when on Saturday mornings I'd unlock the store front door, turn on the spotlights inside the store and pull the sales rack to the sidewalk. I organized and folded jeans and shirts, counted the change in the register as I waited for the first customers. Since this branch of Levi's store was in a neighborhood closer to the train station and the east side of downtown, that is, the seedier part of Oslo, the clientele sometimes reflected that unique urban milieu. It was not uncommon that I had to fend with shoplifters, some whose appearance and behavior betrayed their addiction and hard life. It was not a job for the fearful.

Then there were summers between the ages of fourteen and eighteen, when I left Oslo and headed south for my job at the seaside resort where all the rooms had twin beds, white lace curtains, a wall-mounted white porcelain sink in the room, and a shared bathroom down the hall. Located on the summery island of Tjøme, about two hours south of Oslo, the main building of the Inn was a large, wooden, traditional structure painted white, with paned windows that opened toward the salty ocean in front and an overgrown field in the back. Throughout the building, sheer curtains danced in open windows from the draft of the mild summer breeze.

At the inn I became somewhat of a mascot, being the youngest girl on staff and from "away" (i.e. the city); but also, I was the staffer who knew what table return-guests preferred, what wine they liked with dinner, or what cocktail they would order in the evening; I was the girl who picked wildflowers and arranged them in little vintage cut-glass vases in guest-rooms and on everyone's dining-room table.

Anton, the owner, was the third generation in his family of innkeepers, and I was very fond of him and his lovable personality, especially because I knew how much he and my dad meant to each other. A tall man who wore cardigans and made a shuffling sound as he moved around the kitchen in his Birkenstocks, his face was lined from a life marked by hardship. He and his wife Marianne had lost two infants to crib death, and he struggled with alcoholism. Anton was a gentle giant who loved to laugh and joke around when he was well, but when he was hung over or recovering from a bout of drinking, he was gruff and quiet. Marianne had a shriller personality and was less forgiving, and in her high-pitched voice with a perpetual cigarette in her hand, patrolled the inn and called us out if we didn't vacuum well enough or set the tables correctly. Looking back, I see how her quality control was an important part of running the place, but at the time, her perceptive eyes and exacting critique made us young girls on staff roll our eyes and slink away.

Anton's nickname for me was "the potato." "Nina is as versatile as a potato; she is useful for everything: cooking, cleaning, maid service, reception, waitressing, childcare, chauffeur, and gardener," he'd say. Being called a potato was a compliment, and those hailing from a potato culture like mine will appreciate the comparison. The summers at Tjøme were industrious periods in which I learned about the positive feelings associated with financial freedom, respect, and independence, and having my creative expressions of resourcefulness and energy appreciated and valued.

However, I'm convinced that had I been a child growing up in the 1990s or later, vs. the 1960s and 1970s, I would likely have been diagnosed and maybe even treated for ADHD. Contrary to the social/medical/psychological help offered to kids with attention and hyperactivity issues today—those lucky enough to have the proper support-network and parents with resources—the kids in my generation had to manage with the hand we were dealt. If we were lucky, we were able to develop skills to adapt and compensate, eventually figuring out how to best use these unique character traits and aptitudes we didn't know had a name.

As an adult, I have been floored to recognize myself in the various clinical descriptions of behavioral features typical for ADHD. However, I have also gleefully checked off what I call the positive attributes for adults with the diagnosis. I say, "with glee," because it's a relief to realize that I am not alone, and that on the flip side of the "challenge-coin" are all these wonderfully empowering aptitudes and traits that make me feel proud and, in many ways, privileged.

Recognizing abilities like spontaneity, out-the-box creativity, and heightened energy—ADHD characteristics pointed out by specialists—has felt both validating and emboldening, and true to how I know myself. Adults with ADHD often add pizzazz to romantic interludes and are known for showering their partners with affection, as well as forever believing in the power of love, even when their relationships hit a bump in the road. *Yes, yes, yes, I so am this person, and this is all good!* I nod at the computer screen, engrossed in research on the topic. I immediately copy and paste the information into the body of an email and send it off to Tony, my beloved partner. "See? That's me!" I type, followed by a smiley face.

On the other hand, three typical and problematic characteristics of ADHD are inattention, hyperactivity, and impulsivity and boy do I know these well. Emotional impulsivity often leads to actions like easily flying off the handle or blurting out hurtful things, and I cringe when I think about my ongoing struggles with what is termed "diminished inhibition" leading to hasty responses (and interrupting, one of my specialties), frustration, and impatience. As our couple's therapist points out, "your reactivity." And that's not all: people with ADHD often have impaired executive function and feel emotions more intensely than neurotypical people. We tend to fixate on thoughts and feelings, not being able to shift away from them, be they positive or negative. I mull over these for a while before emailing *that* list to Tony, too. This time without the smiley face, and instead with the added text, "Well, this explains a lot."

A Sisterly Comparison

Tone, my sister and only sibling, is the exact opposite of me, something I used to find puzzling, considering we have the same gene pool and were raised in the same household by the same parents. But of course, our age difference of six years means it was no longer the same household, and my parents were no longer the same—six years is a long time in a marriage and in life. Even if there had only been two years between us, it would not have been the same household energy and dynamics. I've seen this clearly with my own three sons, all born within four years. It's said you can never cross the same river twice. The river, like the energy of our family dynamics, are in constant movement and never at any one time the same river as it was just a moment ago.

When I joined the world in 1965, my parents were newly married and in love, and probably gushing with all sorts of positive vibes. As is typical for most parents of firstborns, they gave me all their attention, and as a baby and toddler I was the center of their universe. That is, until my sister came along in 1972, after my parents had tried for several years to have a second child. In a faded color photo from the day my mom came home from the hospital, she is seated in our kitchen, holding the wrapped-up bundle in soft, pink-striped cotton blankets containing my baby sister. I stand next to her, leaning in, and my smile reveals missing front teeth and cheeks flushed red from anticipation. I had waited a long time for my sister.

I willingly call myself a scatterbrain, whereas Tone is not one at all, except on a rare occasion she'll tell me with no small amount of horror, how she experienced a disorganized or forgetful moment. When she bought a new house that needed total renovation before she and her husband Arild and their two kids could move in (accompanied by their lovable orange mutt and Mallorca transplant named Melis), they quickly and easily sold their old house. For a brief time, they owned both the old and the new which were located two doors down from each other. While work was going on in the new house, they simultaneously prepared to vacate the old, and this timeline could only be changed at great financial cost. Hence, a potentially stressful situation, especially if everything did not go as planned. Tone had a lot going on and not only was she the general contractor and go-to person on-site for all the subcontractors, but also, "naturally," in charge of managing the kids, cooking, cleaning, chauffeuring, food shopping, homework coaching, and last but not least, walking their hyperactive pooch.

Lucky for her husband, Tone was in between "real" jobs, so she could hold down ten others, for free. With each little detail that didn't go as planned on the construction site— and there were many, daily, small and large emergencies and practical problems that needed urgent solutions—her regular sense of and need for order, predictability, and control was put to the test. There were delays, and of course there were fuck-ups. Speaking with me via FaceTime one day while at her wits' end, she wanted to illustrate how maddening it all was, and how all the loose ends and ongoing hurdles and demands made her feel like a disheveled jumble.

"I mean, you know it's bad when this happens," she said, setting up the scene. "I locked the car to run into a store and left the key in the car door!" she continued, exasperated. "Can you imagine? Somebody could have just walked up to the car, and driven away!"

I chortled imagining how she must have reacted the moment she realized her *faux pas*. Tone rarely, if ever, seems frazzled to me; she deals with life and situations in a measured, reflected, and pragmatic way. She is the detached chill to my overly emotionally involved messiness.

"If it's any comfort," I blurted out, "that happens to me all the time!" She laughed, resigned. "Welcome to my exclusive club!" I added, knowing full well that she would rather lose a limb than be included in *this* club: the scatterbrain club where I have a lifetime membership and a record of dedicated service.

To her, a life with this level of absentminded, disorganized condition would be akin to a life in hell. The funny thing is, I think I am the pragmatic chill to my Tony's emotional reactivity. He can easily work himself into a tizzy, and he looks to me for organized calm. Oh, the irony. Reminds me of lesson number one from my late father: Everything is relative.

The Butt of the Joke

Although I think of the three body parts of the brain, mouth, and butt as my up-to-no-good trinity, a scheming irreverent threesome that has often made it challenging for me to comply with behavioral norms, I wanted to give some extra space to the lowliest of the three: my derrière. It carries a few memories from my younger days, independent from its cronies, the brain and the mouth.

Butt Memory #1: Enema

I am about six or seven years old, lying on my belly, prone on a soft blanket on our living room floor. My tush is bare, and my father is standing over me, an image which is probably making you go *ewww* because we're conditioned to imagine the worst about this kind of set up. He is holding up a thick, rubbery, rectangular bag of warm water from which runs a long, see-through silicone tube, the end of it inserted into my bottom. I am miserable, maybe crying or whimpering. I don't recall the sensation of being constipated as a child, but I must have been so and badly, at least this once. I can vividly feel the swoosh of the water making its way into my little body, and that unfamiliar, unsettling rumbling that happens almost immediately as the enema begins to work its magic.

This was in the days before disposable everything, and I recall seeing the enema bag, tube, and "mouthpiece" (the nozzle part inserted into the tushy) later on in our medicine cabinet, as it had been cleaned and was ready for future use, like the rectal thermometer, the ear syringe, and the little glass eye-rinse cup. It amazes me that I remember so clearly the enema séance taking place in our first apartment, that I was on a big, square blanket in front of the TV, and that it was my dad who administered it. (I even remember the pattern of the blanket and that part of the cotton stuffing was coming out of a corner.) I usually lament not having many memories from early childhood, but this is a vivid one.

Butt Memory #2: The Spanking

I don't think his hand lands on my bum with anything more than a few, controlled taps the day my father is trying to teach me a lesson. My parents did not use physical force or violence in raising my sister and me; if anything, they gave me time-outs and consequences such as house arrest for bad behavior. Being confined to stay home, maybe even in my room, meant missing out on cool stuff that was going on in my world outside our apartment; activities, birthday parties, playdates, or *anything happening in the neighborhood*. That was bad enough.

But on the day of the spanking, my dad holds me face down across his lap for a well-deserved *pahtch*, the punishment for my disrespectful behavior. I am about ten or eleven years old, and I have been disrespectful toward my mom—or was it the babysitter? Possibly both—so much so that she (my mom or the babysitter) may even be in tears. I seem to remember sniffles, and not just my own. I was a tall, lanky and moody girl who got into trouble and did naughty things like torture my sister by hiding her toys or taunting her, lying, shoplifting, and running away. I was a defiant, fresh-mouthed kid who loved to push the boundaries of grown-ups I did not consider my friends.

On this day, I had pushed it too far, and my insolence was reported (by my mom or the babysitter) to my dad, who was charged with administering the punishment. But my dad was usually my ally, the adult in whom I would confide, and I can't imagine he approached the task with much energy or enthusiasm, let alone anger or rage. He most likely went along because it was what you were supposed to do, if your kid disrespected adults.

When I grew up, being spanked was never called "getting a beating," the way I often hear my contemporary Americans talk about how adults would discipline them when they were young. Rather, we used the term *ris på rumpa*, a less severe sounding adage, almost playful, meaning "a spanking on the tushy." It appears that, despite the non-violent and controlled circumstance of me receiving this punishment, I must have felt utterly humiliated because I remember both my anger and rage, snot and tears, and lots of sulking. Then there was definitely a loud bang from me when I slammed shut the door to my room. I may have even run away for a few hours, just to make my point. I never ran far—maybe to the park or to the basement of the building next door—and I always returned home when I got hungry.

Butt Memory #3: The Touch

I'm sliding off the exam table at a walk-in state-run health clinic in Oslo, housed on the ground floor of a striking 1920s brick building close to downtown. Wide-open, skeletal legs, the metal stirrups are obscene to my seventeen-year-old eyes. This is my first visit to an OB-GYN.

My parents don't know I am here (remember, they never talked to me about sex or birth control; some 1970s folks!) but my girlfriend Diedra and I have decided to take matters into our own hands and made appointments together. My recent abortion when Diedra was my only confidante and witness was the catalyst for our not-a-moment-too-soon visit to the free clinic. We are also seriously flirting with groovy Jamaican and Gambian dudes at the reggae dance club we have been frequenting on Tuesday nights and anticipate with giddiness what it might lead to. We are excited and buoyant, feeling mature and independent, despite the secretiveness of our mission. At least now we'll be prepared and, finally, responsible.

The male doctor, who is alone in the examination room with me (yup, those were the early 1980s), sits on a low swivel stool, the kind with metal wheels and a black, round, leather seat. The exam is over, and I think *that wasn't so bad* as the doctor pushes back to give me space to hop down from the table. He is friendly, relaxed, and the office is bright and painted in cheery yellow or cream and decorated with colorful artwork on the walls, beautifully framed.

And now, the doctor is going to write me a prescription for birth control pills. A milestone toward adulthood has just been reached, and I am finally feeling like a bona fide adult. My pants and underwear are draped over a chair behind a screen in the corner of the room, where my cowboy boots sit neatly side by side in a small, gritty puddle from the wet and sandy winter sidewalks. As I turn to get my clothes, I feel his hand on my butt and notice that he pats it, while he addresses me.

What is he saying? It might be something benign like best of luck to you or good to have met you, or, maybe, he gives me an off-color compliment or makes a proposition. All that will remain lodged somewhere deep inside me, is that it doesn't feel right that his hand is on my butt, especially after I got up from the table, and the exam was done.

I know I did not think or say, "Hands off, mister!" But why not? This unsettles me and suddenly turns the idea I had of maturity and achievement into something disquieting. This uneasy awareness will stay with me for decades, just under the surface, kind of forgotten, but not.

But then, more than thirty years later, the #MeToo movement's never-ending hemorrhaging of stories of sexual harassment and inappropriate, non-consensual behavior explodes onto social media.

This #MeToo moment of mine was so brief, almost fleeting, and it didn't go further than that touch, or were there several? I wasn't raped or molested. Or perhaps I was molested? Harassed? It was so subtle, so private, so not forceful or grotesque. Or maybe it was grotesque?

I didn't run away or leave in a hurry or even feel scared. Did I think he was handsome? Did I feel as though his touch was a compliment? I won't remember any such details. But that weird, unnerving sensation lingers in my emotional muscle memory. Now, writing about it, I have come to realize that this moment has etched itself in my memory for a reason: It was wrong, and I knew it all along.

Butt Memory #4: Bee-Hind

The day I came running into the wooden ranger's station at Hawk Mountain in Kempton, Pennsylvania, adrenaline rushed through my body while a shooting, needle-prick pain made the bottom of my right butt cheek throb. The three park rangers looked up from their desks, all clad in the tan park uniforms with their nametags neatly pinned to the chest, and the oldest one—maybe in his sixties—had his ranger's hat on and a beard down to his chest. The screen door slammed shut behind me.

I was nineteen and a newly minted au pair, taking care of Pringle and Hank Pfeifer's little prince, their first and only son, the two-and-a-half-year-old, towheaded Henry Charles Pfeifer IV. Hank, my host dad, was an avid bird watcher and this was their traditional pilgrimage to Hawk Mountain where the annual migration of hundreds of bird species coincides with the visual feast that is the iconic and colorful fall of the Northeast. Their Chevrolet Caprice Classic station wagon with wooden side panels pulled their pop-up camper that comfortably slept all four of us. Camping with them was a crash course in Americana and life with a family living in one of the wealthiest towns in all of the US. But Hank and Pringle were refreshingly down to earth and modest. Hence the pop-up camper.

Inside the ranger's station, six eyes peer up at me from behind desks.

"Hi guys, I just got stung," I said and pointed to my lower right side and smiled, almost apologetically. "It hurts a lot and I'm wondering what I should do?"

"I got this," the senior ranger said and rose, sounding in charge.

He approached me and grabbed a first aid kit from a hook on the wall by the door, and kindly asked me to follow him into a separate room "for some privacy."

The surprise of the sting had sent me flying up with a yelp from the wooden picnic table where I hadn't noticed the squiggly yellow and black body of the little fella crawling around the outside edge of the weathered bench. Quickly, the burning sensation spread, and for a second I thought, *I'm not allergic, am I? No, I'm not allergic. Not allergic. Calm down,* while hyper-acutely paying attention to the adrenaline making its speedy rush through my body. I must have surprised the wasp, or was it bee?—I couldn't tell the difference— just as I was about to sit down to enjoy a packed sandwich lunch with my American host family, surrounded as we were by majestic mountains in reds, oranges, yellows, and browns during this peak foliage season.

The bearded grandpa ranger closed the door to the room which had a tall wooden bench along one wall, the kind in doctors' exam rooms, but without the fake leather and crisp tissue paper cover. He nodded in the direction of the bench.

"Well, I'm going to have to take a look at that, then," he said, sounding professional but also kind, aware of the delicacy of the situation due to the sting's location. Suddenly it dawned at me that I had to drop my pants in order for him to inspect the wound. I sighed.

"Sure," I said and turned away from him, my hands tugging on the waist line of my sweats. "It still hurts like hell," I continued, as if to fill the awkward space of momentary silence.

"Oh, don't you worry, we see these all the time," he comforted me, as I felt the cool fall air in the room brush over my pale-fleshed bum, facing him. Thankfully, the rest of the bee-sting visit is utterly uneventful. In light of how quickly and easily this type of situation can go from okay to awful for a young woman alone in an exam room with a man, I'm happy for this uneventfulness. However, doesn't it strike you, as it does me, as lamentable that this is why it stands out because it didn't take a turn for the worse?

When I returned to the picnic table and told my host parents about the enthusiastic first-aid offer at the ranger's station, Hank's laughter made his big torso and belly shake. He enjoyed my candid descriptions and sense of humor, and I in turn loved to make him laugh. I heard the sound of Pringle giggling before saying something advisory in the way she would often respond. We cackled a lot together that year, my host family and I, and the friendship still endures today, some thirty-five years later.

On Managing the Imperfect Trifecta

Sometimes while at the movies, or in a social gathering, I burst out in loud, raucous laughter, as I am known to do. My brain registers a fleeting funny or glorious instance, be it on screen or in a told anecdote, and my mouth immediately takes over without delay.

The laughing gear just goes, "Hey, I've got this! I'm just gonna explode here!" and a joyous roaring sound escapes from my lips. Predictably, the boyfriend or the son(s) are bothered by my sudden and gregarious outburst. I say, *Too bad, get used to it, this is who I am and whom you love! Don't scold me or ask me to be someone I am not* (i.e. meek, quiet, shy, and invisible). They will shrug, roll their eyes, and cautiously check to see if anyone else is reacting. (Usually, nobody is, or if someone is, it's typically with a smile, not a growl.)

My girlfriends love what they call my contagious, raucous laughter and the fact that I feel no shame in expressing myself genuinely in the moment. But I admit I sometimes hear myself several noise bars above everyone else in the room, which makes me wince just a wee bit. A girlfriend once told me she had trouble with me because I "take up so much space." She did not mean that my physical body was too big— it was all about my too-large personality as she experienced it, passionate and unreserved as it can easily and suddenly be, and I've come to understand that this is not necessarily easy for everyone to be around.

But I don't really know how to be different unless I try to be someone who is not genuinely Nina. I have shared these thoughts with my now first and only ex-girlfriend, (girlfriends break up too, you know), and even suggested that if we can't be ourselves without hurting or annoying the other, perhaps it is time to let the friendship reach its natural end, that this must be better than asking or expecting the other to change for our comfort. I would not want her to try to be someone that is not really who she is, in order to please me, or not piss me off.

Similarly, I think back to my failed marriage and wonder if perhaps my sometimes-intense emotional exhibition and reactivity might have been too much for Dan to deal with. "You take up a lot of space in the sun," he once said; he wanted to be the one in the spotlight. During our divorce, he told me he preferred a woman who wanted to be his shadow.

Well, good luck with that, I thought. "What will she do when the sun sets?" I asked. He didn't have an answer.

Dan was patient and quick to forgive, whereas it was difficult for me to let go of things that bothered me, to stop obsessing and brooding, and to insistently re-address a point he had long let go. I see now, how I might have been "too much," and it hurts to imagine this trait of mine as a possible and maybe even potent player in the demise of my marriage.

Once, when my mom visited me in the States when I was young and newly married, but before I had kids, we spent a fun and loud evening around the dinner table at my in-laws. During the hour-long drive back to my place, she told me she didn't understand how I held my own in their company, since they were so vociferous, often interrupting each other, laughing and making fun, roasting and teasing as well as arguing. It was normal fare in the Lichtenstein Jewish tribe, to let it all hang out; everything and anything was up for grabs, and I had grown to love it, even find a place to belong *in* it. This was quite different from our Scandinavian way.

Chez nous, God help you if your elbows were on the table or if you chewed with your mouth open or made that smacking sound while chewing your food.

At the Lichtensteins' table, *smatting* (a great Norwegian onomatopoeia for that wet, mushy sound that is heard from chewing with your mouth open) was a sure thing, as was eating straight from the serving platter, and unabashed finger-licking.

Sometime after having established her firm opinion about my boisterous in-laws, my mom once scolded me for interrupting her, saying I had to stop the bad habit. To my defense, I think I had assumed it as a tactic in my Lichtenstein Tribe Survival Strategy. But also, now that I have read so much about ADHD and the common traits associated with it, I realize that interrupting is one expression of the typical lack of impulse control. Interruption management is something I have been working on, as my tendency to interrupt indiscriminately has also been my partner's most significant relationship complaint. The ADHD brain that I identify with is so high energy and so easily distracted that in the middle of listening to someone else speak, when a thought comes to mind in response to what is being said (but not always on topic), waiting my turn usually means losing the thought. In the moment, waiting doesn't seem like an option. It's as if a gate or boundary is missing, one that would remind me to hold back and internalize my thought and store it close to the surface but wait to verbalize it until the other person is done talking. It. Is. Just. So. Difficult. To. Do.

"Breathe in slowly, count to eight, hold your breath for four, then, breathe out slowly for eight."

I am in my yoga class, practicing mindfulness and relaxation, as well as physical flexibility and strength. Yoga has helped me become a better version of myself on many levels, but especially with regards to self-awareness. Together with biking, swimming, kayaking, and hiking, activities part of my (usually) regular routine, yoga encourages my mind to slow down and to notice both the interior and exterior world with a kind of calm and compassion I don't naturally experience. It seems this quiet space is critical for me because I am easily overwhelmed by people and sounds that require me to pay attention. Spending time by myself in a meditative type of movement becomes a restorative act—redemptive, even.

At the end of each yoga class, when the body feels warm and supple, and the mind feels calm and unoccupied, we assume the position of *shavasana*, or corpse pose. In this completely restful posture, prone on our backs, palms facing up and eyes closed, feet relaxed with toes loosely turning out, I imagine myself blissfully dead, and relish in the minutes of a weightless, unattached state. With nothing cluttering my body or mind, I think, *if this is what it's like to be departed, I will not be afraid when my time comes.*

For it is only during *shavasana* when my usually overcharged mind and often-shallow, reactive breath don't burden my body and my being. *This is not a bad place to end,* I think. As the yoga class wraps up, seated cross legged on our mats with our hands touching in front of our hearts, the teacher leads us in a brief *metta* or loving kindness mediation: "May all beings be safe. May all beings be happy. May all beings live in peace." *Namaste*, he says, and bows. *Namaste*, I say, and bow back in a gesture of gratitude.

Heart

There is nothing more whole than a broken heart.
Rabbi Menachem Mendel of Kotzk, Poland

My life has not involved trials by fire, tragic, or what I think of as traumatic events by any standard definition. My parents loved me, I had a safe home in a peaceful country, and I never experienced natural disasters, violence, war, illness, or abuse. I migrated out of my own free will from one rich country to another. There was alcohol, a lot of alcohol, as my parents were serious partiers in the sixties, seventies, and eighties, and I was a classic latchkey kid, but those family stories are not harrowing, although they, too, have affected my sister and me. This, I particularly have come to understand as I have explored my body for embedded memories: trauma does not need to be on a grand, violent scale to leave its effects and imprints.

After a safe and relatively privileged childhood came international travel, then higher education, scholarships, love, finding a home in the Jewish tribe, marriage, and three healthy children. All marvelous blessings. *Booooring*, the sabotaging voice says.

But then came a series of big bangs.

According to author and social critic Debora Copaken, "heartbreak is not just an apt descriptor of the way we feel when we lose love. It is also an excellent physiological description for our body's reaction to the shock of that sudden loss. Worse, that feeling of brokenness in the center of the chest doesn't just go away. It sticks around ... Make no mistake about it: Losing love is trauma."

Aside from the big bang heartbreaks of mid-life, my heart has broken a tiny bit every day since my childhood when I was—like all children destined to become writers—"a particular genus of angelic spy," as Jayne Anne Phillips notes in her essay "Outlaw Heart." But as writers, "we might one day intervene in the dynamics of loss, insist that sorrow not be meaningless," she adds.

That sorrow not be meaningless. *How can these heartbreaks be redeemed?* I think. *Who can release me from this ache in my core, other than myself?*

.

Heartbreak # 1: Losing Pappa

My dad didn't die when he was supposed to, which made us happy. For eight years after his lung cancer surgery, Tone and I felt we had him on borrowed time, and we relished this with acute appreciation, humbled by what we saw as a great privilege of gifted time together. This didn't make his eventual death any less of a heartbreak of course, but we couldn't say it wasn't expected. Nonetheless, when the reality hits me of not being able to hold his hand again or share a beer over meaningful conversations about life or see him interact with my sons, grief swells within me. Molten hot and liquid lava rises and soundlessly moves through my body, until I have to heave for breath, overcome with sadness.

In 2004, he was sixty-nine and diagnosed with one of the most lethal beasts of cancer, which didn't surprise anyone, since he had smoked upwards of forty cigarettes a day for forty years. When my sister and I learned about his diagnosis, it was already past tense.

"I had some lung cancer," he said when Tone finally got a hold of him on the phone after he had been MIA for about two weeks. He had not wanted to worry us, his two daughters with their young children and full lives: one in Oslo, the other in the States, so far away. We lost our breaths at the thought of him alone in the hospital but respected his preference and decision not to tell us in advance. I've wondered what it must have been like for him to receive the diagnosis, alone, yet not having wanted to tell us, to share the news and talk about it. I think of him taking it in, realizing what he was up against, and withdrawing to deal with it on his own: a wild creature in nature who when he senses his own sickness and impending mortality, goes off from the herd to heal or die alone.

At that point he and our mom had been divorced for about five years, and he was on his own, living a vagrant life, temporarily camping out at friends' places, not really working much save for some house painting and handy-man gigs. After his cancer diagnosis, he had driven himself to the hospital, undergone the surgery, and was in recovery when my sister finally saw him. Lucky for him, there was no chemo, no radiation; they just took out his entire lung and hoped there was no spreading. Which there wasn't. Naturally, the words "lung cancer" made us think that *that* was going to be it, a swift death sentence, but Pappa beat the odds, against all odds. At least for eight years.

When death came for him, in the early morning hours in late October 2012, he fell to the floor next to his bed where my sister later found him in a small pool of blood from the fall. The night before, she had come over for dinner, and although he didn't eat anything, he had a beer while my sister enjoyed what he had prepared for them. They chatted and she later told me he had seemed weak, but as always relished her company as she did his. After my sister left that night, his last night of life, he had cleaned up after dinner, washed the dishes and put everything away.

When he had not answered his cell phone the next morning, even though they had agreed to speak, Tone said she already knew. Turning the key in the lock to his ground floor one-bedroom rental apartment, she braced herself for what she might discover. The apartment was neat, not one thing out of place. Except our dad.

I believe he was ready, and having just seen my sister, who was home for a visit from Mallorca where she lived at the time, must have given him permission, so to speak, to let go. He had been struggling more than usual the last months, breath labored, sleepless nights, no energy. I was scheduled to come home a month later, over Thanksgiving break from my teaching job at UCONN, and had spoken to him a few days earlier, urging him to hang on and look forward to our time together: a light in the northern darkness. But his light was already dimming, and he knew it. We knew it too.

When Tone called me that day, she said, *nå er pappa død*, "Pappa is dead now," the "*nå*" or "now" separating the theoretical event of his death which we had carried close to our hearts in preparation for so long, from the inescapable presence of the sudden reality. Our generous, loving, complex, and eccentric dad had left this world, left our reach. I hovered outside my body, cortisol rushing through me from head to toe, my heart racing. He was gone.

My dad's ashes were scattered in the Norwegian Sea a few nautical miles offshore by a lighthouse that meant a lot to us, with a pod of seals looking on with curious interest from a nearby rock.

"Make sure you do it with the wind blowing away from you," he had joked when he was still alive, when we talked about his wishes of having his ashes scattered in the ocean by his buddy Anton's inn at Tjøme. The idea of not being eternally stuck in one place appealed to him, and so Benya held the urn snugly in his lap as the open-hulled wooden boat made its way out to the spot on the horizon that my dad, my sister and I had agreed on.

On a day with impossibly blue skies and gentle winds for the late northern summer, my dad's fisherman friend Kåre Karlsen had offered to be the captain and take us out on his traditional fishing boat with room for ten on benches lining the bulwark. We tried to remember my dad's advice about the wind, but some of the fine dust still rose toward our nostrils and mouths when we gently shook out the sometimes-lumpy content of the urn landing on the water's surface before sinking into the deep. I didn't mind the minute remnants of my dad clinging to my clothes and eye lashes while I helped my son and niece each have their turn scattering their grandfather's remains in the ocean.

·

It took my sister and me all of one day to clean out his small efficiency apartment after he died; his earthly belongings were few and mostly consisted of books and some clothes.

His favorite hat ended up in my middle son Gabi's room, and Benya still wears his winter coat. Tobi, my bookworm son, brought a stack of his grandfather's books back the States, Kurt Vonnegut among his favorites. I have my dad's briefcase with a collection of old letters and cards I have written him since I moved to America in the 1980s, and a scattering of photos I have sent him of my boys over the years. It breaks my heart to sift through them; a lifetime of separation and love, staying in touch and connected in the best way I could. In a vintage cigar box tied closed with a ribbon, we found a stash of letters dated from 1957, written in beautiful cursive hand-writing with blue ink and signed, Sissel. His first love? She must have been special since he kept the letters all those years.

Aside from his five grandchildren and a large group of good friends who loved him despite or perhaps because of his marvelously unique brand of personality, it's his uncompro-mising love and affection for my sister and me that remain with us. That and a few good tales is the best anyone could wish for. My oldest son, a writer, has penned stories about his grandfather; is there any better inheritance?

That sorrow not be meaningless.

Heartbreak #2: Losing Husband, Marriage, and Home

When Gabi, our thirteen-year-old, heard the news, he stormed out of the living room, ran up the stairs, and slammed the door to his bedroom.

"Give him some space," I said to Dan, putting my hand out to signal he should remain seated. The lump lodged in my throat and my stomach since I woke up that morning suddenly swelled, and adrenaline rushed through my arteries, causing that surreal, out of body sensation.

Fighting back tears, Dan was more somber than I had ever seen him. Benya, who was twelve, sat quietly on the rug intently fiddling with a puzzle on the coffee table, eyes turned downward. *Did he even hear what we had just told them? Was it sinking in?* He seemed detached, zoned out. Tobi, just about to turn fifteen, was on the couch and had turned away when he understood what we told him and his brothers, his back facing us now, his knees pulled up to a fetal position. His hands were in or near his mouth. I heard whimpers.

All the guilt and sorrow around my divorce are gelled into this one heartbreaking moment: the moment I had to tell our boys that their lives would never be the same again.

Our little, precious tribe of five, our inimitable Viking-Jewish clan, was gathered as if in council, seated on sheep-skins from Norway in front of the fireplace in our living room, when my husband and I were to announce the revision plans for our family, toward an unhappy ending. The once gracious and welcoming living room, where I had myself painted the tall, elegantly paneled walls in warm mustard gold, suddenly felt cold and cavernous. No longer a space for raucous and fun-loving gatherings with family and friends, all the laughter was gone.

We waited in silence a few minutes for Gabi to return. He must have been hurting behind his slammed-shut door, maybe sprawled on his bed, face pressed into his pillow, over-whelmed, and confused. Eventually Dan got up, his large frame filling the French doors to the hallway, and climbed the creaky, grand stairs to retrieve our normally spirited and lanky teenager from his room. Still no sound from Benya, our pensive one who always takes his time. He kept at the puzzle, his sweet, round face turned down, his dexterous fingers patiently trying to fit a new piece of the complex puzzle that maybe had become more difficult by the news he seemed to not, but must have heard, not looking up even once.

Soon, Dan and Gabi rejoined the sorry bunch of us, and we tried to resume the conversation, which was not a conversation at all, but an awkward attempt at damage control from sad news. Suddenly, Tobi exclaimed, "You can't get divorced, we are the Lichtensteins!" rolling back over to face us, his cheeks wet from tears, his nose dripping snot.

"I thought you were going to tell us we were having a baby," Gabi muttered. Slouched in his chair, crestfallen with his arms crossed, his eyes remained fixed on the floor in front of him. Dan and I were speechless.

Earlier that morning I woke up queasy, only able to take shallow breaths. Dan and I had agreed that it was time to tell our boys. We had been in crisis mode for too long, and we were exhausted. I believe we were both eager to move on, away from the pain, the frustration, and the isolation we felt pulling each of us under in our own, lonely experience. I don't understand how it could be that we were ready to let go of this most precious thing we had, our family, and to this day it remains my biggest regret: I think we thought about ourselves before our kids. Instead of putting on our hard hats, rolling up our sleeves, and tackling the complex and time-consuming soul work necessary for possible repair and recovery of trust in our couplehood, we bailed. *Selfish bastards*, my inner critical voice says. After many hushed and not-so-hushed conversations and arguments, and with Dan's ongoing insistence that a trial separation was not an option since he didn't want to "give the kids false hope," I eventually conceded. I know that Dan suffered with this as much as I did, but his mind was made up with much more resolve than mine. The fantasy of healing and reunion still flickered in me. I wanted it extinguished but I couldn't help but nurture this stubborn, tiny flame, notwithstanding the repeated hurt this would cause me.

That morning Dan was quiet, withdrawn, and spent a long time in the bathroom.

"I can't do it," he said as we were getting dressed quietly in our bedroom. "You're much better at formulating things. You have to be the one to start the speaking …" We still slept in the same room, in the same bed—a California king mattress on the hardwood floor—through the mess of it all.

Our beautiful cherry-wood Ethan Allen bed frame had literally crashed to the floor in what I had come to see as no subtle metaphor for the state of our marriage.

"You have to tell them. Tell them we agree, that it's our decision together," he added.

I agreed and I did not. I hated him and loved him. I pushed him away, repulsed, and I drew him near, scared and unwilling to let go. He comforted me and he wounded me, and I him. On the mattress on the floor in our bedroom, we blamed each other and told each other hurtful stories of lies and deceit, but we also made love. That was the truth of our last chapter.

Throughout the morning, I felt like an executioner on his way to make heads roll and bodies slump. Lives end. There are many ways to deliver a devastating blow. How could I articulate the imminent end of the safe and comforting world as our boys knew it? I didn't have a manual, mentor, or doula for this, one of the most harrowing but common life-cycle transitions imaginable. I wanted to push off having to tell them, as I hoped that I might wake up one day to find my husband pining for us to heal and reconcile. How romantic! How optimistic! How naïve ... I would have jumped at the opportunity to do the work with him, for us, for our family, but I'm still not sure I fought hard enough, or with sufficient conviction. I was not selfless enough. I was not willing to sacrifice enough.

In our living room the day of the announcement, we made promises we did not keep. *We will still be a family even though Mamma and Pappa will not be married. We will still celebrate holidays and birthdays together. We will still ... We will still ... We will still.* But we were never the same again.

That sorrow not be meaningless.

Heartbreak #3: Losing my Tribe

Suddenly, everything was quiet, but the void was loud and echoed like torture. From one day to the next, my raucous, recently turned ex-in-law family no longer answered my emails or returned my phone calls. The colorful invitation to the Hanukkah children's party my sons and I were organizing for their little cousins in my new, post-divorce condo, remained unanswered. The party was cancelled. Mother-in-law, father in-law, and two sisters-in-law had decided to cut all ties with me after twenty-six years of serious tribal bonding. They were hurt and angry about things I had said and done during the complicated time of my separation and divorce from their only son and brother. I was devastated that they were not willing to forgive. *For the sake of the children,* I said.

Dan and I agreed that we had behaved in ways we were not proud of; we had experienced up close and personal the fact that a marriage breaking up provokes less than stellar reactivity in the wounded and hurting parties. But we had also agreed that we should focus on the positive things we shared, especially the love for our three sons and the gratitude for each other as parenting partners. His family did not seem willing to share our perspective and chose instead to delete me, what they considered the source of their hurt and disappointments.

My ex-in-law family was an unusual Jewish clan—a loud, fun-loving, tight-knit group whose car and truck-windows displayed NRA stickers, and who carried tubs of Lysol wipes and Purell hand sanitizer long before Covid-19. To them, family was everything, and they protected it—as well as their property—from intruders and strangers with love, dedication and overprotective fervor (including guns). At the entrance of the long, curved gravel driveway on their rural Connecticut property, a rustic hand-made sign read, "Nothing sold here. Back out now." My ex-mother-in-law was not your run-of-the-mill *bubbie* because this matriarch carried a thirty-eight caliber in her handbag and swore like a trooper. Nor was my father-in-law your everyday *zaydie*; he did a hundred push-ups and a hundred pull-ups in his basement every morning before 5 a.m., and on his days off he'd be packing a Smith & Wesson in a leather holster, driving a tractor in his fields while smoking fat cigars. Their greatest enemy, after public schools and their "liberal brain-washing agendas," was the ubiquitous germ in all its imaginable permutations. Despite their eccentricities, I grew to love them deeply. Father-in-law baked the best bialys ever and mother-in-law gave selflessly of herself.

It must have been a shock to them when, in the summer of 1985, I—the braless, Scandinavian, nationally programmed socialist that I was at nineteen—introduced myself with a firm, confident handshake. I was five feet, ten inches tall, fair-haired and blue-eyed, outspoken and independent, and on my handbag were a variety of buttons: Bob Marley in Rasta colors, a peace sign, a pink women's liberation fist, and a reminder to "Party Naked!" My guess is they privately hyperventilated, and I don't mean in the same way their son had when we first met a few weeks earlier.

Although not observant by any Orthodox standards, my mother in-law taught me by meticulous example not only how to make the clearest chicken soup, the fluffiest matzo balls and the most tender brisket, but also how to prepare the Passover *seder*, and make the High Holidays meaningful. With me, she gained a third daughter, one who was eager to learn, asking many questions along the way. Soon, my in-laws went from being kosher style to seriously kosher, and when I converted they offered me an inscribed *siddur* or prayer book, thanking me for having enriched their Jewish lives.

We gave them their first three grandchildren, and my Viking genes were welcomed as they bolstered the Eastern European gene-pool and gave them improbably blond-haired babies to call their own. Due to my orthodox conversion, their grand-sons' Jewish identities would never be questioned, and hence, their own legacy of Jewish continuity secured.

The relationship with my in-law family was not always silky smooth and without squabbles, but if there was tension it was in that stereotypical, suffocating-but-loving-in-your-face-driving-you-crazy-we-will-always-stick-up-for-one-another-loud kind of way. I still feel my mother-in-law's soft and generous bosom as we'd hug, and the warm reverberations of the laughs we'd share over drinks at their kitchen bar still make me smile. I cherished all the practical life-advice and deeper conversations I could count on having with my father-in-law. He was knowledgeable and wise, and if we caught him at the right time, he was disarming and goofy. I grew close to the sisters-in-laws not so much because we were alike, but because we shared a family and a deep love for Judaism and family traditions. The girls were larger than life, both in mind and matter, with lots of opinions that they didn't see any reason to keep to themselves. But I was no meek little lamb either. They expressed their love as their presence in the room: generously. Twenty-six years of sisterhood ended abruptly after my divorce, and it is a loss I am still constantly aware of, although the ache has diminished slightly as each year goes by.

When I learned from my boys that their grandmother had Alzheimer's, it saddened me that I could not be there to support the family in the predictably difficult years ahead. I sent letters extending olive branches on various occasions but never received any response. Even if no reconciliation is possible, I hold an immerse gratitude for all that we shared. I would not be who I am today without them.

That sorrow not be meaningless.

Ears

I'm hypersensitive to sounds and if asleep I'll wake up from the pitter-patter of mice and men alike. For this reason, I often sleep with foamy earplugs pushed deep into my ear canals. Despite this sensitivity when I need quiet in order to sleep or read, I think I am actually challenged in the hearing department when I move about in the world. I don't mean that my hearing is physically debilitated, but rather that I am (too) easily distracted, and that this diminishes what I'm able to hear. For example, if there are many different sounds going on at the same time, like water running in the sink while butter sizzles in the pan and my iPhone emits dings from incoming texts, emails, or Facebook notifications, the moment feels way too audibly busy. Add someone speaking to me at the same time, perhaps while I'm trying to find my place in a recipe or count tablespoons, and I am quickly overwhelmed. My acute hearing is dependent on my ability to pay attention, so it makes sense that it's at night I hear best, when all quotidian distractions are absent.

Late one midsummer night in Oslo, right when the mere hour-and-a-half of almost darkness reminds Norwegians that summer won't last forever, I am biking home from a friend's house through a wooded area. I am about fifteen. Something brings me to a stop on the path, and standing on the soft ground where layers of old greeneries rest soft on moss and dirt, I hear the sounds of creeping and crawling from under the leaves.

The moon shines through the dense treetops, magically lighting up patches on the ground around me, and the leaves are moving! I rest my bike against the trunk of a tree and kneel down on the dry, brittle leaves, listening and looking, my ears and eyes and every cell of my body hyper alert with the kind of extreme openness and receptivity that is turned on when a person has to navigate through darkness.

The closer I get, the better I hear and see the movements. I now realize it's happening everywhere around me; I focus my gaze on the ground in concentric circles moving away from my spot, and see the leaves rustle and budge to the sound of a whole world of tiny creatures—night crawlers—busy living their lives. I think I even hear them chew.

Mesmerized and giddy with awe, I bike home marveling about this living ecosphere and can't wait to tell my dad. I always loved to ponder questions of life and death with my curious, autodidact father, and so the next day, he willingly drives us to the magical spot. He pulls over to the side of the road and I hop out, leading the way to the leaf-covered ground. I'm a bit disappointed since it looks a lot less magical in daylight, but standing there quietly with dad, both of us breathing as quietly as we can scanning the ground for signs of life, is thrilling in its own right. But there is nothing but the sound of birds chirping in the treetops and passing cars on the nearby highway.

"Well, that's why they call them nightcrawlers," my dad says while he gently pushes some leaves aside with the tip of his sneaker, exposing the underlying dirt. "You can see the traces here from their emerging from the ground." He points to small mounds of soil and tiny holes. I push aside some sticks and leaves where I stand and find the same signs of the nightly feasters.

Although this nighttime auditory experience in the Oslo woods may not seem particularly unusual—after all it was a naturally occurring phenomenon that was far from unique or rare—there was something about it that embedded itself in my emotional memory. I believe it could be that it happened at a particularly existential time during my impressionable teenage years when I often struggled with philosophical conundrums and the marvels of the natural world, and I loved that my dad showed interest in my nature experience and my hungry curiosity. That he took time to accompany me back to the spot to investigate with me, made me feel seen and heard by him. There was perhaps a certain intimacy I experienced with him that day that speaks to how special a moment this was, where he was so fully there for me, and only me. Thinking back, I imagine all the trees surrounding us as witnesses to the father-daughter bonding that was ours right then, and that must have felt singularly perfect, and all I ever wanted.

My ears picked up on another memorable nightly feast forty years later in France, where Tony and I are at an Airbnb flat in the Bastille neighborhood of Paris. It's the second time we have rented from Adrian, a South African expat whose apartment has an airy open floor plan—a chic space with Chesterfield leather couches and floor-to-ceiling windows, facing a lush green courtyard.

It's late at night and Tony is asleep in the bedroom while I battle jet lag trying to read myself tired in the living room. I sit on the firm leather sofa under the floor lamp light and slowly turn pages while I hear Tony's steady breathing from behind the closed pocket doors—antique wood carved in an intricate pattern—that separate the living space from the bedroom.

Suddenly, squeaks sound from the open kitchen area opposite where I sit. I continue reading, not sure what it might be, but a few minutes later, something tiny darts by on the floor in my peripheral view. The book rests open on my lap while I keep an intent lookout for suspects. I hear the scurrying again and a tiny brown mouse zooms behind the planters in front of the windows.

There's definitely more than one, I think, as I rise and quietly approach the kitchen wall at the other end of the living room, determined to discover the whereabouts of what must be their high-pitched chatter. I'm absorbed in my mission as I listen, holding my breath. What might I hear or see next?

Quiet. The wrought iron gate to the shared courtyard opens and closes; a cat meows in the distance, but there's no mouse conversation. Ever so gently I begin to pull open drawers and cabinets where food is stored, and as I slowly tug on the second drawer and peek inside, dozens of little, brown mice scamper out of open cracker boxes and chip bags, and in less than three seconds, all that is left from their midnight feast in the drawer-mess-hall is a scattering of itty-bitty black poops.

I can't help but smile as I throw out the crime scenes that were the open cracker boxes and chips bags; the mice were so cute after all. But I won't deny that had they been rats or had the apartment been mine, I would probably not have been so charmed by the culprits and their home invasion, caught as they were *in flagrante delicto*.

.

I love to play loud music. Some of my happiest hearing memories are from when my kids were young and I would put on a CD or an LP, crank up the volume, and the boys and I would dance and twirl and run, exhilarated, through the house. Our favorite was an LP in my records-stash from Norway, Edward Grieg's *Peer Gynt Suites* No 1, Op. 46, "In the Hall of the Mountain King."

The piece starts in a slow and rhythmic, thumping beat, with just a few string and horn instruments playing in an explorative staccato, *bam-bam-bam*. The boys and I become the trolls that inhabit Norwegian forests and mountains, and move in slow motion, our arms out wide and our steps big and heavy, faces stern and twisted on our tilted, bobbing heads. As the measures pass, a few more strings join in, picking, and more wind instruments like flutes and clarinets and oboes enter, and we escalate our pace too, exploring the corners of the living room, around the couch, and in front of the fireplace. Our two Lhasa Apsos follow us. Wanting in on the action, they sense the rising excitement and nip at our moving feet. The pace increases until more and more of the orchestra—all the strings, all the winds, the cymbals, and the drums—join and we move faster, the dogs underfoot, and circle the dining room table and run through the kitchen and back out to the living room, where the tall floor-speakers stream out the glorious music. The volume and the pace increase again when the strings become more assertive, as do the wind instruments, the clarinet, and the trombones, and the thumping rhythm quickens and the sound gets deeper and more dramatic.

At about two minutes in, with only forty seconds to go, the entire philharmonic orchestra is playing, every single instrument, and the tempo and intensity reach a crescendo in a frantic mass of loud, explosive, symphonic uproar that makes us run and twirl faster and faster and faster, until in synchrony with the last, grand bangs of the bass drums and the final loud gong, we collapse together on the floor in a heap of exhausted troll bliss.

"Again, again, again!" Gabi shouts between giggles, while Benya makes a funny face, sticking out his tongue, and Tobi rolls his eyes and moans, exhausted. But we pick our sweaty bodies up and do it one more time, and maybe even again. My little Norwegian trolls and I storm through the house to the sounds of Grieg's "In the Hall of the Mountain King," whose wild and boisterous symphonic ride I will always associate with the unreserved delight we shared.

Feet

The human foot is a masterpiece
of engineering and a work of art.
Leonardo da Vinci

I am almost seventeen years old, standing in a small shoe store on the French Riviera bravely asking in my high-school French to try on a pair of beautiful orange suede sandals. I am here with a group of Norwegian girlfriends for three weeks, attending an immersive language program.

The salesclerk—a petite woman with a pointy nose and narrow, red lips—says, "*Oui, bien sûre mademoiselle, quelle est votre pointure?*" Of course, miss, what size do you need? *Grande*, I say in French, around forty-two, with a repentant look, as if apologizing for my feet's Nordic size to these delicate Mediterranean creatures.

The woman looks at her colleague. The two of them don't move an inch, just shake their heads emphatically. Through tight smirks they inform me that they never have a women's size *that big.* My girlfriends stand outside the window chatting while they wait for me. None of *them* wear a size forty-two; all of them look fabulous when topless on the beach, sporting golden tans (I am sunburned) and colorful bikini-bottoms tied low at the hips, while swarthy Latin men in Speedos circle them— famished, greedy falcons hovering over prey. None of my girlfriends have to worry about being taller than the studs lining up to court them, nor about having bigger hands and feet than the boys they have crushes on.

Just as I am in between generations—Gen X and Baby Boomers—so am I in between shoe sizes, 10.5 and 11. In the US the average women's shoe size is 8.5, so that's how stores plan their inventory. I typically see a cool design or color I love, only to be swiftly informed that the store doesn't have that particular shoe in my size, or that in my size, they only have black or brown. *Black or brown? Really.* So much for orange shoes. Often, I have ended up with the men's version of a shoe, and soon feel lumpy and unsexy, filled with regret for having spent money on something that doesn't bring me joy.

That means no cool purple curlicue trim on my cross-country ski boots (also available in apple green in women's sizes); no multicolored neon sneakers. *Feh, the neon is only a fad anyway*, I try to comfort myself. My father would have reminded me that the trendy people would have to renew their shoes as soon as the style was outdated. I, on the other hand, could keep mine for years to come, if I took good care of them. My dad taught me how to polish shoes and boots "properly" (horse-hair brushes with wood backs, only) and to stuff them with newspaper if they got wet inside.

When I started dating at sixteen, I was super self-conscious about having larger feet and hands than my boyfriends. At parties, I noticed that when all our winter shoes were piled up inside the front door of the hosting home, mine were huge compared to the other girls and blended in with the boys' footwear. Once, when I was in a rush at home, heading out and unable to find my shoes, my dad called from the living room, "You can borrow mine!" I did not think his teasing was funny, which is probably why I remember it so well.

It was a great relief that when I met Dan when he was twenty-three, he was tall like a basketball player and had hands the size of XXL catcher's mitts and feet the size of canoes. Next to him, I could wear high-heeled shoes and still felt feminine and almost petite, and not as gargantuan as the heels made me. However, the problem with Dan's idea of my feet, and feet in general, was that he pointed out how gross he thought it was that I had a few short, blond hairs growing on the middle digit of my big toes, and told me I should pluck them, something I found to be not just insulting but also ludicrous. He was a compulsive plucker himself and could constantly be seen with tweezers in hand, removing itty-bitty hairs from his own fingers, toes, nose, ears, and any other appendage where he thought hair didn't belong. (remember "Teeth" and the code red when food was detected in between cuspids? Same concept, different body parts).

Writing this, I realize how grateful I am that today, I no longer have to feel paranoid about being criticized or corrected about what in my first marriage were considered bodily imperfections. Thanks to Tony's more generous and naturalistic approach to the human body, its appendages, and functions, I feel loved, appreciated, and desired, regardless of my extra pounds, the occasional seed caught between my teeth, and toes with hairs. In fact, it's I, now, who has to be mindful of not picking on him for the very things Dan used to point out and that made the overly sensitive me feel badly about. What a moment of self-awareness: realizing the importance of the age-old adage and golden rule, "do unto others as you wish they do onto you." Bam. *Live and learn, Nina,* my conscience speaks to me. Live and learn and be grateful for the wisdom you are able to harness with every day that goes by in this precious life.

Today, my honey and I wear the same size shoes, his hands just a little fleshier than mine, my fingers longer than his. I also stand taller than him at my 5'10" to his 5'7," so, it has worked out well that I've come to prefer lower, more comfortable shoes to the high-heeled "fuck-me-pumps" (as Amy Winehouse called them) of my younger years.

I don't mind so much anymore that my feet are rather large for a woman and get this: growing! Apparently, this is common after having pounded our feet for half a century or more, with ligaments and tendons stretching and getting loser (yeah, yeah, I know, not the only part of my female anatomy distending and loosening these days). Some women can expect their feet to grow half a size every ten years after the age of forty, which for me could mean reaching size 13, if I live to my nineties. A size and age to behold.

I glance down at my deep wine-colored toenails and like what I see: feet that look lovely despite their size, thanks in no small part to the pedicures I afford myself in the summer months, and I'm grateful for these nicely shaped, thus-far-strong limbs. My feet continue to serve as solid foundations as I move through life, stepping through mundane tasks, yoga poses, pedaling my road bike, chasing my dreams and adventures, seeking out loved ones, moving across state-lines, country borders, oceans, and continents as they carry me, step by step, without trouble or complaints.

Hips

these hips are big hips
they need space to
move around in.
they don't fit into little
petty places. these hips
are free hips.
they don't like to be held back.
these hips have never been enslaved,
they go where they want to go
they do what they want to do.
these hips are mighty hips.
these hips are magic hips.
i have known them
to put a spell on a man and
spin him like a top!
"Homage to My Hips" Lucille Clifton

One night, the summer of my fifty-third birthday, I limped and moaned my way to the bathroom in the dark, my right hip in agony. *Cancer!* was my first thought. I had recently lost two dear women friends, both way too young to meet their premature demise. If these two women could just up and die from such aggressive and ravaging diseases, then what's to say I wouldn't?

Back in bed, struggling to find a comfortable position, I pondered the hip issue and my worst-case scenario thoughts, but slowly managed to calm my overactive imagination with slow, mindful breathing. The pain probably had to do with the extra thirty pounds I'd been lugging around the last few years. Comforted by my poundage (who knew?) I imagined, *tomorrow I'll start making healthier lifestyle choices.*

I thought how this should inspire me to bite the bullet and hold off on those heavenly Maker's Mark Manhattans at the end of the day that Tony and I love to share in the winter, or the refreshing gin and tonics we relish in the summers. Of course, enjoying these libations made my (otherwise weak) ability to control portions go straight to hell. Why have one piece of cheese when you can eat the whole cheese?

Rose hips don't worry about how big they are, writes Gayle Brandeis in her book *Fruitflesh.* "Why should you care about the size of your hips?" she asks. In my younger, fertile and childbearing years, I was told more than a few times that I have good hips for carrying babies. Typically, these unsolicited comments came from women so insignificant in my life I don't recall their names, but I understood I had childbearing hips.

This, I surmised, was just a way for someone with body image hang-ups to find a functional reason for what they might have considered my wide hips. I, on the other hand, never had a problem with the girth of my *coxa* in my youth, and even now, when my softer and more generously shaped hips require larger and looser clothing to be comfortable, I still consider them a healthy part of my body that I, mostly, appreciate. It probably doesn't hurt that Tony often both tells me and shows me that he loves my hips when he touches and caresses their curvy outline and generous, warm expanse, dips, and inclines in ways that give me as much pleasure as it does him.

"Write about your hips. Exult in their fleshiness, their rhythm, the movements they allow. Tell the truth about your hips." Brandeis urges me on. Then she reprints Lesléa Newman's "Ode to My Hips," and encourages her reader to also write an ode to her hips, so I try.

Ode to My Hips

Forty-six inches of pure female power,
I make no apologies, I do not cower.
These hips have chutzpah and need their space,
They give me the confidence I wear on my face.

I place my hands on these two hips,
As I'm not one into pursing my lips.
But I enjoy that confident womanly stand,
Feet slightly apart, in front of my man.

Behold the curves, the wealth, and the dips,
I tell you, these are truly womanly hips!
They think they can change the world! —they kill!
Unlocking all sorts of creative juices at will.

Steadfast through gestation, childbirth and more,
My hips are a body part I simply must adore.

They might be outspoken, but I honor their voice
and let them speak the truth. Do I even have a choice?

So, thank you, my darlings, for keeping me sound
Your steadiness holds me close to the ground.
I don't take you for granted, I hope you know that,
And reward you I will, on the yoga mat.

"Any requests today?" my yoga teacher Leslie asks at the beginning of class while we are seated cross-legged on our yoga mats at 7:30 a.m. This early in the morning, my hips are tighter than later in the day.

I often think of how I want to approach aging as Leslie has. Her hair is cropped, reddish and curly, she wears no make-up that I can see, and her short body has soft curves visible through relaxed, cotton clothing. She is different than many other yoga teachers I have taken classes with—young women with super-thin bodies, sinewy arms and legs, tattoos, and the latest designs in colorful, tight-fitting yoga wear. Many of them will allude to body-image and control issues from their pasts, and it becomes especially evident from the readings or inspirational talks they share before or during our practice that they have found their healing in yoga and now love sharing their inspiration and path to health with their students.

Even though I have been lucky so far to avoid any serious body-image issues or eating disorders, it's always good to hear about the importance of loving our bodies and how to listen to our emotional needs through mindfulness in practice, as on the mat. I don't hate my body or find it problematic, though lately (ha! As in the last ten years!) there seems to generally be more of me than what we are told is optimal for health. But since my penchant in general is to be hypercritical of most things, I always welcome and nod in recognition when we are coached to love, support, listen to and heed our body's needs and messages. I inhale and try to carry with me into my daily life off the mat the mind-body awareness and compassion toward ourselves with which yoga continues to enlighten me.

During class, Leslie smiles and laughs and sighs and moans, in that yogi kind of way that encourages presence through breath and movement and mindfulness. Her sounds also make it less awkward for us students if or when we omit noises, be it a yelp from pain during a bend, or a grunt from an awkward stand, or if a fart escapes while we stretch. The twice a week yoga practice I try to maintain is a much needed and dedicated time to mind as much as my body, to connect with all of myself in an uncluttered, compassionate, and guided environment. To me, *this* is much needed therapy.

"Hip openers!" one woman calls out from the back of the room.

"Okay, hips," Leslie echoes back. "Anything else you want to give some extra attention today?" she prods us on.

"Shoulders ..." the guy to my left mutters, as someone else chimes in with a "Yes, shoulders! They're super stiff from gardening!"

"But definitely hips," I add, heeding the tightness of mine after all the hours spent seated in front of my computer screen, typing away, or lately, on board airplanes in transatlantic crossings, cramped in tight seats for too many hours on end. I already anticipate how much suppler they'll feel at the end of class and smile to myself.

"Well, just when we thought spring had finally arrived in Maine," Leslie says, "it got cold again, and we tighten up and get protective in our bodies. We need to loosen this all up!" We nod and mumble our recognition and appreciation in unison. "So, let's find a comfortable seated position, let your hands rest in your lap, and gently close your eyes ..." She sighs, breathes deeply, and we are off to an hour of delicious and much-needed mind and body nurturing.

When we come to the hip opening stretches, it's difficult for me to relax and breathe into the soreness and resistance I notice. I want to regain smoother mobility because I know that when my hips are open and happy, the benefits reach far beyond their physicality. The hips, represented by *swadisthana* or the sacral chakra, is the second chakra of the seven most often referred to in Western yoga practice, and is located just above the root chakra and below the solar plexus chakra.

Over the years I've understood that the sacral chakra is connected to a sense of abundance, well-being, pleasure, sexuality, and creativity. I have also learnt that this chakra is all about my connection and ability to accept others and new experiences. So, when I am easily irritated at my partner or other people's behavior, I don't just remind myself of Carl Jung's wise saying, "Everything that irritates us about others can lead us to an understanding of ourselves," but also realize my hips need work. I definitely want my *swadisthana* to be in balance and am convinced that it will be beneficial to both my writing and relationships. So, I stay in the hip-opener poses just a little longer than when Leslie invites us out of them and try to visualize the blood flow and oxygen as they regenerate the lushness and mobility of my beloved hip region.

Thanks to yoga I have gained a better understanding of, and appreciation for, my various body parts, beyond their purely physical existence. I'll continue to drag myself back to the mat even in the darkness of winter mornings through ice, sleet, and freezing temperatures because I crave to fertilize my body and mind with the wisdom and benefits inherent in the practice.

Leslie closes our class with a *metta* mediation which often makes me well up in tears as it evokes a sensation of being deeply connected to all beings. We are back to sitting cross-legged on our mats, and I notice that this pose is a tad easier for me now, compared to at the beginning of class. Our hands are in prayer position in front of our heart chakra and our eyes are closed as she closes our practice with the traditional, "Namaste."

Belly

In the days and weeks after the birth of each of my sons, I'd look down on my belly and find it alien. My tummy was mushy and big and made me wonder if it could possibly contain another munchkin? Nobody told me about *that* part of the childbearing process—the post-partum lumpy bleeding, the lingering cramps, the unfamiliar shape of my body, despite the baby being out. I was lucky to be able to nurse all three boys, as this turns out to be nature's way to expedite the maternal body's return to "normalcy." Except, of course, there is no "return," just a new normal, which is one of the hardest but also most valuable lessons that applies to most things in life.

My three boys each greeted the world more or less the size of a typical three-month old; round cheeked and chubby from day one. I still can't quite fathom how this kind of emergence can be a safe and natural process; Gabi, my middle kid, was the most humongous, weighing in at almost twelve pounds! I had a fabulous midwife and no drugs. This whole thing still blows my mind.

As life happens, it takes its toll on a belly, not just from childbearing, as probably most middle-aged women *sans enfants* can attest to; we're in this never-ending morphing business together. Observant Jewish living has meant a lot of lavishly prepared and rich—too rich—Sabbath and holiday meals, and since the Sabbath comes *every* week, without fail, it's impossible to skip it. From the sweet and yeasty challah bread, to savory noodle and potato kugels full of oil, to meats of every kind, stuffed, baked, simmered and stewed. And on Shabbat it's not just one dessert, but several, and who can take just one piece of chocolate babka or rugelach? Or skip dessert? Let me tell you: it's impossible, to me.

My waistline, hips, and belly kept expanding a little after each year, after each baby, and although I've always been physically active and exercise regularly, my weight hit an all-time high at the same time Dan hit his midlife crisis.

My father was recovering from lung cancer surgery in 2005, just as I turned forty and was about to finish my PhD. The convergence of these three events felt momentous, an urgent call to action: my dad's life so imminently threatened, and mine, so definitely mid-way (if I'm among the lucky), combined with the completion (finally!) of my doctorate after many years of postponing the last hurdle—the dissertation-due to childrearing; I had earned an adventure.

"Pappa, I have an idea," I said on the phone, fighting back tears, relieved my dad had pulled through the surgery okay and didn't need chemo or radiation. He now had only one lung, but since there was no metastasis, his prognosis was better than most lung cancer survivors.

"How about I come home to Norway with the boys for a year, so we can spend some quality time together?" I hoped the prospect of having us near would give him something tangible and lovely to look forward to. That this promise of time spent together more easily and frequently would boost his spirits and help him heal. Make him want to live and thrive for us, with us. With me by his side, finally.

"Really? Oh honey, that would be something special," he said. He was emotional as well; I could hear it on his breath.

I don't remember what came first, me mentioning to Dan I wanted to make a year in Norway happen, or me making a promise to my dad. I do know I was not going to be dissuaded; this was one of those existential moments when you just know in your heart it's the thing you must do to live with yourself and not have regrets.

So, I brought the boys to live in Oslo for a year. Dan agreed reluctantly to my going, ceding to my wishes because he knew how much my dad meant to me and how important it was for our boys to get to know him and my mom better. Dan and I always said we'd go live in Norway for a while, so that our kids could become comfortable in my culture and language as well, but his business made it impossible for him to plan any long-term absence from the US. Me taking the kids for this one year seemed to me like a fair compromise, and now, what with my father's serious health scare, I felt time was of the essence.

Dan was supposed to "commute" to come see me and the kids in Oslo about every six weeks, but he never traveled easily. It took him a long time to get over jet lag, and he'd often catch a cold on the plane that he'd nurse the whole time during his visit. Add all the frantic prepping in order to for him to be able to leave his business for ten days, coupled with the never-ending catching up when he returned, and the "every six weeks plan" made it an impossible commitment for him. This was before the concept and logistics of remote work were as easy as they have become today, and especially after the Zoom explosion we have seen since Covid. The result was that months went by without us being together as a family.

Meanwhile, alone at home in Connecticut, he used his newfound free time to turn himself into a chiseled Adonis at his dojo, practicing and teaching Brazilian jiu jitsu, his beloved and newfound passion. To his evolving new look, he added a soul patch (the small patch of facial hair just below the lower lip is also known as a *mouche* or a jazz dot) and wore red bandanas or Under Armor black spandex skull-caps over his shaved bald head. With his six-foot four-inch 260-pound frame, he made for an impressionable presence.

About mid-year, I was waiting for him with butterflies in my stomach at the airport arrivals, enjoying the sight of loved ones reuniting with smiles, sighs, and joyous squeals. When Dan finally walked through the electronic double doors, I felt a sudden heat flush my face. I always loved when we'd meet at the airport after a separation; it was a new and exciting discovery yet a grounding reunion with familiar smells and touches. This time it felt different. The man who sauntered toward me was a different person and I could tell something was off right away.

"Look at you!" I said in surprise, measuring him up and down. I couldn't make myself compliment his svelte appearance in his soul-patched, bandana wearing macho state. Something hit me in the gut as a turn-off. It was stronger than my normal attraction to him; it was as if we were the two equal sides of magnets that when put together, repel each other.

Despite my initial visceral reaction at the airport, we had a sweet homecoming at our apartment as the boys returned from school and found their pappa on the couch with a great big smile and open arms. After the kids went to bed, he ran his big, strong hands over my hips and belly, a touch I typically loved.

"Why didn't you get rid of this excess?" he asked, measuring my curves with his eyes and grip. "Didn't you say that life in Norway would be super healthy, and that you'd get into shape?"

I mumbled something about not having time to work out since single parenting and diving into a new, full-time job as a teacher was at times overwhelming and consumed all my time.

"These love-handles aren't exactly a turn on, you know," he continued. A wave of defensiveness came over me and disgust for how he carried himself. *A clown*, I thought, fuming. I took my pillow and blanket and slept, wounded, on the couch that night.

The next time my belly is flat as a pancake and the love handles gone, we are separated and in the process of getting divorced. I'm "skinny" and get lots of compliments both from Dan and my surroundings about how great I look, but of course, I feel like shit. I wake up with stomach aches in the morning and go to bed numbed from too much wine or bourbon or both. I get through the day with the help of Zoloft and Xanax. I even added Ambien to the mix at night to ensure at least six hours of oblivious rest, since though the alcohol put me to sleep with ease, I'd wake up in the middle of the night with insomnia and a racing heart. I had become a beautifully skinny, miserable, forty-five-year-old woman.

It was during this wretched period that, for the first time in my life, I forgot to eat regular meals, and lost so much weight that I fit into my size eight wedding gown for the first time since 1988, when I was twenty-three. I recall how awesome *and* how awful it felt when the zipper of the Laura Ashley brocade and Basque-waisted dress from the 1980s closed with ease, and I morbidly decided to wear it to my synagogue's Purim carnival party, equipped with a cardboard sign around my neck that read: Mail Order Bride.

"Wow, you look fabulous!" people exclaimed. While the world around me offered enthusiasm and positive feedback about my appearance, I was never more broken. The drugs sailed me through the emotional fog with a chemically induced glow.

.

Ten years later, as I'm watching the fourth episode of *The Crown* on Netflix, my hand runs over the softness of my middle-aged belly, bloated after my partner Tony and I have enjoyed a dinner of veggie burgers with melted Swiss cheese and oven-baked sweet potato fries. I sip an Allagash White straight from the bottle, while Tony pours his into a stemmed glass, letting the foaming head reach past the top of the glass, just the way he likes it. I'm slumped comfortably on the couch next to him, as Queen Elizabeth's coronation is about to take place on the screen with much pomp and circumstance. My belly is covered by the light cotton of my long and comfortable, shapeless summer dress.

My hips and stomach are the two areas of my body over which I feel the least control; these are the body parts that have morphed into their own independent nations during the throes of menopause, as if a riotous and expansionist tyrant is at the helm, oblivious to how her megalomania is making the rest of me feel about my ever expanding, physical borders. Where will it all end?

Perhaps it's time to act. But that will require the full cooperation of all parts of the body-nation, especially the control tower up top, which for some reason has of late proven to be disturbingly laissez-faire, in favor of a gluttonous enjoyment of life's edible pleasures. *What the heck is this all about?* I am tempted to ask, but in fact I know already: women my age (let me remind you: more than fifty, less than sixty) often arrive at a point in our lives when we decide it's not worth the battle anymore. Let bellies be soft and bulbous, hips wide and grabbable, underarms wobbly; life is too short to struggle where no struggle is needed, especially if the goal is mostly to please everyone else but ourselves. So just pass the Montepulciano and the camembert, will you?

.

I'm sitting at my new primary care physician's office; it's our baseline, "get to know you" exam, and he's asking all the routine questions about my general health, habits, and family history. He asks me how much I weigh, (because it doesn't say on the chart that the nurse handed him, the chart she held on a clipboard when she called me from the waiting room and where she was supposed to take notes from the height, weight, and blood pressure thing they do before the doc enters the exam room; absence of noted weight to be explained below) and I say, "too much." He doesn't look up from the chart, and instead asks, "Ok, tell me about what you do for activities?" I begin to ramble off all the physical activities I enjoy on a fairly regular basis: yoga, hiking, biking, kayaking, swimming, skiing, and then he interrupts me with a half-smile and says something that initially shocks me, as much as it tickles me: "So, you're fat and fit, nothing wrong with that." *Fat and fit*, I think, and while I chew on the doc's choice of health identity label for his new patient, he continues: "Research shows that as we age, it's better to have some extra weight as long as we stay active, so you're good." *I am good*, I think, trying to imagine that an expression about myself that has the word "fat" in it, can be a good thing, that it can be something I can embrace and perhaps even come to own and love.

Lately, I've taken to decline stepping on the scale when the nurse calls me in from the waiting room because I'd rather not be reminded of the digits I've grown resigned to accept as the new, post-menopausal but also happy-with-my-life me. (It's enough that I must deal with my no-longer flat belly which insists on stubbornly following me around), You see, I have discovered that I can say, "no thanks" when prompted by the often a-little-too-chipper nurse or CNA, and that she accepts my "no" as if it was the most natural thing in the world— imagine that! Of course, I realize when I don't have the choice not to record my weight, for example when going for a colonoscopy and the health team needs to know the correct figure for them to administer the appropriate amount of anesthesia (a lot!), something I appreciate very much. Or, when I recently checked in for a flight on a wee eight-passenger Cessna plane from the quaint airport in Lancaster, PA, and the first question the woman behind the counter asked me was how much I weigh. I couldn't help but burst out laughing while mumbling something like, "I guess this is not the time I should lie about my weight, uh?" She didn't smile, her pen waiting midair. I took a deep breath and told her the actual truth, and she didn't wince (I mean, why would she?), which made me feel a little better. I also felt better knowing the plane would be balanced and the flight safer by the crew deciding who should sit where in distributing the poundage accordingly.

By the time I returned home after my annual physical check-up cum meet-and-greet, I had decided that "fat and fit" was a tolerable truth, even one I wanted to try to make peace with. In classic, impulsive Nina fashion, I promptly created a Facebook post about this new status of mine, which of course was nothing new at all, since I had been fat and fit for many years by now, but there was something empowering about saying it "out loud." I added an artsy and whimsical illustration I had seen online of large-bodied women in leotards and yoga wear in all sorts of flowy poses and hit "post." Within hours there were over a hundred likes and some forty comments from women who thanked me for sharing my body-positive experience. It felt good to share, and it felt great to know I was heard and seen and not alone.

Big belly, flat belly, pregnant belly, post-partum belly, soft belly, ripped belly, post-menopausal belly; I've known them all, intimately. With all my body work and body thinking in writing this book, I have come to respect and feel gratitude for this steadfast partner of mine, despite—or perhaps because of— its independent spirit. I've also humbly discovered, in my research, that this belly, this gut, plays a profoundly important role in my ability for deep, instinctive understanding or feeling. And this, dear reader, infinitely ups my appreciation for its alliance.

A few years ago, I received a myofascial massage, which targets the thin connective tissue, known as *fascia*, that surrounds and wraps most structures in the body, like our organs, bones, muscles etc. It's believed to be helpful with relaxing contracted muscles, improving blood and lymphatic circulation, and is often used by osteopaths and in alternative medicine to restore balance in the body. A lot of the session was spent manipulating my belly region, home to our most vital organs, and it was not always so comfortable when the therapist's hands pressed, rolled, and kneaded this self-aware section of my anatomy. But what I learned that day about this fascinating thing called fascia has only strengthened my belief about how our body is not just the most reliable source of our knowing, but also the most underappreciated, according to traditional Western medicine.

Keep in mind that especially since the Enlightenment and the seventeenth century, when the philosopher René Descartes developed the so-called "rationalist system of philosophy" as epitomized by his dictum, *cogito ergo sum*, or, "I think, therefore I am," the body was replaced by the mind as the seat of all existential knowledge and "proof" of existence and "reality." The human body, contrary to the henceforth esteemed mind, became associated with decay, the irrational, the female, the evil, the impure, and the weak (take a pick, right?), while thought and intellectual abilities represented truth, clarity, masculinity, power, purity, and eternity, in other words, what to value, what to strive for, what to idealize. Add to that the Puritan and body-denying Christian tradition that has dominated Western cultures for centuries, and we can understand how it has come to be that the body has lost its "standing" as a valuable, or *invaluable*, source of knowledge and understanding of human experience.

The well-known trauma therapist Bessel Van Der Kolk, author of the now seminal work, *The Body Keeps the Score*, noted how this misplaced emphasis effected his work: "I discovered that my professional training, with its focus on understanding and insight, had largely ignored the relevance of the living, breathing body, the foundation of our selves." Only when he began to consider the "breathing body" of his patients, and not just what was going on inside their minds, was he able to help them heal from their past traumas. I might go out on a limb and say that not until I took the leap to consider involving the breathing body of 'me', was I able to reconcile my past, which helped me understand … a lot. It is exactly by examining my body's responses, emotions, experiences, and muscle memories, that I know how I have become who I am today. So, sorry, Descartes, but I chose to abide by this dictum: *sentio ergo sum*, I feel therefore I am.

Fascia, it turns out, has more nerve endings than our brain, and thus has an unparalleled ability to perceive and record our experiences, as we move through life. When we say, "I have a gut feeling," about something, this is not just some hokey or superstitious expression, but an actual way our body communicates stored knowledge. We all know how our bodies can communicate and respond to situations that are unsafe, threatening, or triggering. Or joyful and delicious, for that matter. What I have discovered through the humbling journey of listening to my body in writing this book, is that the body knows a shit load of things that the mind is not even close to conceive of in the same innate, instinctive way. And this, dear reader, is an immeasurably valuable and trustworthy resource to be aware of and treasure in life. The hippocampus, that tiny bean-shaped part of the brain, may *think* it's all the hot shit for where memories are stored ("encoded" and "consolidated" as the medical term goes), but your fabulous and spatially impressive body *knows* this is where the action is, was, and always will be.

I have a gut feeling you find this to be a really cool thing, too.

Epilogue

The wealth of information contained in the physicality of the body seems to me as something sacred; sensations that tell stories from one singular life across an expanse of time, there—all over us, around us, in us —for us to mine. Not for the sake of mining alone, but so that we may come to understand how, why, when, and where we became and become who we are today. For the stories already exist, inscribed at a cellular, visceral level, and I consider it sheer and incomparable bravery for us to listen to, transcribe, and make art from the recognition of our own becoming.

Here's how I find the magic of buried memories: I consider the specific body part for a moment, in stillness and with breath, and let it become a meditation exercise. If I can look at it, I focus on its physicality: the structure, the shape, the way the skin looks, the scars, the dimples, the wrinkles. Then I visualize the shape of the body part. Whether I can see it or not, I let curiosity guide my awareness toward the inherent muscle and emotional memories it carries. Usually something comes to mind, and as soon as I begin to write about it, more often follows, bubbles rising and floating up and out toward awareness and recollection. Or, perhaps, the sensation is more like noticing a tiny, focused light whose diameter and reach slowly expands in a space that until now was pure darkness. The more I linger there, with the light as guide, the more it expands its reach, enabling me to grasp not just a specific moment or sensation from that moment, but the space around it, or events that led to it, or followed it.

A revelatory movement into time and space, at its best, it can be glorious, like time travel: I am with my dad again. I'm twelve and he is cleaning the cut on my knee under running water at our kitchen sink. The way he lifted me up. He is my hero. At its best, it can also be extremely painful: the limp, helpless feeling when I fall to the floor as my husband tells me he won't agree to a trial separation, only divorce. The way the wood floor creaked under the weight of my body. The fleece bathrobe I wore protecting my knees. It is suddenly so vivid I shudder and need to get up from my desk to walk and breathe and calm down.

When you mine your body for memory riches, you don't necessarily need to sit, but you do need to listen and be curious. Just like you can do a meditation seated or walking (or lying down), connecting with your body requires you to be present with it, which means to listen inwards. Imagine a busy junction inside you where magic happens, where neurons and muscle cells connect, creating experiential energy you, and only you, can tap into. Steer right into that fertile crossroads and linger a while.

When I want to recover life experiences relative to my hands, for example, I start by looking at them. I turn them this way and that, searching for physical markings or signs of life experience: wrinkles, dimples, bumps, scars. *Ah, that's from when the jagged edge of a can of dog food cut the tip of my index finger to the bone.* Suddenly, I'm in my old kitchen from over twenty years ago, and my three little boys stand around me, awe-struck, as I lean over the kitchen sink splattered with bright red blood, while our neighbor, an emergency room doc, numbs and sews me up. It is as if I am living the moment all over again, and it's rich and vivid and marvelous, despite the searing pain and gushing blood.

After considering my hands' physical appearance, I try to be curious about what they have been part of, or caused, or prevented. I ask myself, "what's a sensation I have loved in these hands?" Immediately, something comes to mind: the way it felt when my sons were little and would hold my hand, and I theirs. *How different each one felt in mine! The way they held on reflected their individual personalities. And when they grew older, how much fun it was to arm wrestle with them, until they all beat me and it was useless to even try. The howls, the sweat, oh the joyous defeat!*

Then, I prod deeper yet: "what's a sensation that was unpleasant for these hands?" I punched a man in the face, once. He asked for it. The story, which I now feverishly write down since it's all there, a scene in an unwritten movie begging to be captured, is hilarious. Drunken young women (my sister, best friend, and I) out on the town (in 1990s Oslo) taking matters (being insulted by a middle-aged asshole in a fancy suit) into their own hands.

It's through this mining work that I have been able to bring awareness to the experiences of my body parts beyond the appreciation of their pure utilitarian function: how my ears enabled me to hear my dogs bark when they wanted to get back into the house, shivering in the rain, their wet snouts leaving trails on the glass panes of the door, or how I listened to my baby babble to himself in his crib, my ear pressed to the door of his room.

I've discovered gratitude for my body parts' more evocative abilities too, turning forgotten incidents into vividly remembered scenes—like when I glance down at my feet, they remind me of the humiliation I felt when asking for a size ten in a shoe salon on the French Riviera because the petite *mademoiselle* clerk (the bitch) laughed out loud and conferred with her associate about my savagely undainty Viking feet. Or, when I check my teeth in the mirror and I recall the way my oral hygiene-obsessed ex-husband parted his lips in a forced smile, pointing to food stuck "between your lateral incisor and right cuspid," making me think, *what the fuck*, during what I thought would be a romantic dinner, instead an emotional turning point in our marriage.

But most of all, listening to the stories my body parts whisper (or scream) has allowed me to observe life a little closer, in order to better understand how I am who and where I am, today. I will even go as far as to say that this exercise, this journey of bodily discovery, has opened my eyes and heart and mind: Because of it, I am able to honor and truly own what has been—bless it even!—and this, in turn, reminds me that it all matters in the construction of my being, and that my life, despite how insignificant and brief it can seem, matters.

Body Memory Prompts

I have found that something magical happens when I turn my attention to a specific body part, for example my hand, or knee, or ear. Maybe you're interested in trying, too?

Below you'll find prompts you can use as take-off points for your own bodily journey of discovery. I hope you'll enjoy conversing with your body parts and that your inquiries will reveal life memories, great and small, maybe even forgotten ones. Let your body show the way in this important journey that is so uniquely yours, and let it be a grounding connection between you and your past experiences, which can often seem ephemeral, and your future, which is, after all, built on our past. Listen patiently to its whispers as it guides you toward your stories, and let these stories bless your life, even though you may feel as though your life has not been blessed. Yet.

The prompts don't follow any particular logic, they are simply different ways that can help you get the conversation going with your most trustworthy partner who always keeps the score: your body.

Eyes

- How would you describe your eyes, physically? Give as many telling details as you can to help us see them.
- If you wear glasses, how are they (or not) an expression of you?
- Are your eyes problematic in any way? Do they cause you grief?
- Think about the very first time you laid eyes on someone you came to love deeply. A partner, a child, a pet, a friend? Describe that moment in as much detail as possible.
- What are ways you like to be seen, or not seen?
- Is there a specific moment or time you witnessed something you have not shared with anyone? Why do you think you have not yet talked about this?
- Have your eyes ever gotten you in trouble? Have you seen something forbidden?
- Have you had an experience where you were observed by someone else, but that you wish could be unseen?
- Do you see things not readily visible to others, things that are not of the material world? If so, explain what, how, when?

Nose

- How would you describe your nose, physically? Give as many telling details as you can to help us see it.
- Describe some smells that transport you, where to and why there? Be specific in details as it helps to build a good story.

- Do you like the shape of your nose? How would you describe it to a non-seeing person?

- Have you ever lost your sense of smell? If so, what was that like? How did it alter your experience of that moment/day/time?

- Imagine you permanently lost your sense of smell. What are some scents or smells/fragrances you would miss the most, and that you would want to be able to imagine and fantasize about. And how would you do that?

- Make a list of the top ten (or top five) smells you absolutely can't stand. That make you sick. Give a sentence as to why you feel this way about each one.

- Pick five random things and free associate with the way they smell, and what that brings up for you. Example: an orange, cinnamon, Play Dough, fresh cut wood, earth …

Mouth

- How would you describe your mouth, physically? Give as many telling details as you can to help us see it.

- Do you sometimes blurt out things and then regret them? Any particular memory of this?

- A wet, cold sweet ice-cream cone. A salty chewy piece of meat. Greasy truffle French fries? Crunchy hard candy? Do you have a specific edible and oral memory?

- Do you mouth off easily? Or are you more prone to keeping your mouth shut and let others do the talking? Have you ever surprised yourself one way or the other?

Ears

- How would you describe your ears, physically? Give as many telling details as you can to help us see them.
- Do you hear certain sounds better than others? Why do you think that is? Selective hearing can be useful …
- Do you wear art in your ears, and do you use your ears a way to express your personality, through accessories? How so?
- How old were you when you pierced your ears? What is the memory like?
- What are sounds that mean "home" to you. Or your sounds of travel? Or sounds of a particular holiday? Or, are there sounds you associate with a person? Give as many details as possible in describing these unique sounds.
- Have your ears given you problems? If so, how?
- Are you a good/bad listener?

Skin

- How would you describe your skin, physically? Give as many telling details as you can to help us see it.
- Does your skin "talk"? That is, can you think of ways a specific memory or situation of your inner life or your well-being is expressed on your skin?
- Do you have a scar, a tattoo, a piercing? Talk about how and when you got it, share the most salient, visceral moment as it happened. How do you look at the scar/tattoo/piercing now, compared to the time you got it. What has changed?

- Talk about a time you feel that you've been "stretched thin," when you were pushed to your limits. Can you appreciate the elasticity of your "skin" (your being/personality/patience?)
- Are you thin-skinned or thick-skinned? How so? Is there a particular situational memory that can demonstrate your level of sensitivity?
- If you have been pregnant and given birth, how did the experience imprint itself on your skin?
- Do you have moles, birthmarks, age-spots, pigment spots? If so, how have they impacted your life? Is there a particular memory associated with them?
- How does your skin react to the sun? Did you ever have a bad sunburn? What happened?

Teeth

- How would you describe your teeth, physically? Give as many telling details as you can to help us see them.
- Have you ever had dreams of your teeth falling out? Why do you think that might have been?
- How do you feel about going to the dentist, and why do you feel the way you do?
- Have you ever bitten anybody? Have you been bitten? What happened?
- When you were little, did you believe in the tooth fairy? Why or why not?
- What do big, white teeth represent to you, and how do you see your own teeth?
- Have you ever had major dental work, and if so, describe what it was like, what you thought about, how you felt? How it changed you.

Hair

- How would you describe your hair, physically? Give as many telling details as you can to help us see it.
- What's your relationship to your hair? Do you spend a lot of money/time on it? Has it always been this way?
- Have you ever suffered from hair loss, and what was that like? Was it during a particular time of your life?
- Have you tried or worn a wig, and what was that like?
- How has your hair changed during the course of your life?
- Do you use your hair as a way to express yourself, and if so, how?
- Talk about what a "bad hair day" means to you.
- Do you have a favorite hairdresser or barber? What's so great about that person or your relationship, and how would you describe a typical appointment? Or, a memorably atypical one?
- Have you ever felt pressured to wear your hair in a particular way, or to cover your hair?
- Do you cover your hair in your daily life (for religious reasons or other reasons) and if so, talk about what this means to you.

Heart

- What/when/how was your first heartbreak?
- Is your heart healthy? Does it ever ache? If so, why do you think that is? And what do you do to make it feel better?

- Have you ever noticed your heart beat or thump so hard it felt like it was coming out of your chest? Describe that situation/memory.
- A time when your heart felt so full it could burst?

Brain

- Does your brain tell you stories? Torture you? Soothe you? Fool you or guide you? Is there a recurrent or obsessive story you carry in your mind? What is it and why do you think it's there?
- What do you do to improve your mindfulness? Or, if you consider yourself a mindful person, was there a time when you were not, and how/what changed and why?
- Talk about your capacity to remember and recall. Are there certain memories you are more likely to remember more clearly than others?
- Are you forgetful? Absentminded? Tell a story about a time/times when this was problematic, or perhaps a blessing?

Hands

- How would you describe your hands, physically? Give as many telling details as you can to help us see them.
- Have you used your hands to defend yourself or someone else?
- What have you built or created with your hands? Broken, or torn down?
- Do your hands hurt you?

- Are your hands strong, and if so, write about the ways your hand-strength has been useful, or shifted over time.
- What are your favorite things to hold in your hands? Or, to let go of?
- Do your hands have scars, and if so, what are they from? Describe what happened.
- Have your hands stolen something? Returned something?
- Do you play an instrument with your hands? Explain how your hands work to make music.
- What's your favorite, or memorable, hand(s) to hold in yours? How so?

Feet

- How would you describe your feet, physically? Give as many telling details as you can to help us see them.
- Do you like your feet? Why or why not?
- Your feet carry you places. What are some of the favorite collaborations in experience you've had with your feet?
- Do your feet give you problems? How so?
- Do you have a shoe fetish? If so, why do you think that is? Explain how it impacts your life.
- Do you like to have your feet massaged? How do you care for your feet, to keep them healthy and happy?

Knees

- How would you describe your knees, physically? Give as many telling details as you can to help us see them.

- Have you ever felt "weak in the knees," and if so, what was the situation?
- Are your knees strong, weak, achy? How does this matter to you?
- Did you ever have an experience which "brought you to your knees"–either literally or metaphorically?
- Our knees are vulnerable as we often land on them if we fall. Do your knees have scars that tell stories?

Back

- How would you describe your back, physically? Give as many telling details as you can to help us see it.
- What burdens have you carried in your life, and how might they relate to your back?
- Back injuries are common, and are often a symptom of a lifestyle choice or a particular event or accident. What stories does your back carry?
- Does your back have certain specific strengths? Weaknesses?
- We sometimes say, "I've got your back." What does this mean to you and do you remember a time when someone had your back, or you theirs?

Butt

- How would you describe your behind, physically? Give as many telling details as you can to help us see it.
- How do you like your butt? How does your butt help you, serve you, protect you?

- Has your butt been the recipient of unwanted/unwarranted touching? How did you deal with that at the time? Would you react differently today?
- Anne Lamott's mantra, "Butt in chair," is on most writer's minds. How do you manage (or not) to make time for writing, or, to sit in meditation, or just quietly sit? What is the value of this for you and what might your challenges be in this?
- Did you ever get spanked on your butt when you were a child? What stories do your butt-memories carry?

Belly

- How would you describe your belly, physically? Give as many telling details as you can to help us see it.
- What stories would your belly tell, if it could talk?
- Did you know that the organs located in our stomach region are covered in facia, a thin casing of connective tissue that surrounds and holds every organ? This thin film is filled with more nerve-endings than our brain. It may just be that our belly is the central station of our "knowing;" our ability to understand; not the brain. So, think about when you have "trusted your gut" or followed your gut feeling." Any particular situations come to mind, when you tap into this very visceral and often uncanny experience?
- Do you like your belly? Has it had different iterations throughout your life? Think about how it has changed over time, and what these times in your life signified.

Hips

- How would you describe your hips, physically? Give as many telling details as you can to help us see them.
- Have you ever been hyper aware of your hips? Describe the situation.
- How have your hips served you well?
- Has anyone made unsolicited comments about your hips?
- Have your hips ever pained you? Ached? Did you know why? Did you imagine/guess why?

Breasts

- How would you describe your breasts, physically? Give as many telling details as you can to help us see them.
- When did you first wear a bra and what was that moment like for you?
- What does it feel like if or when you do not wear a bra?
- Describe one (or several) of your most memorable moments, involving your breasts.
- Have you nursed a child, and if so, what was it like for you when it ended? When it began?
- If you were to tell a young girl what it's like to have a mammogram, how would you do that? What if the description was for a group of women readers/friends, and you could take a funny or irreverent approach, how might that sound different? Speak from your own body-breast memory.
- Are your breasts important for your sexual pleasure? If not, why; and if yes, how? Has it changed as you have aged?

- If you are a guy, how do you think about your breasts? What are some things you might imagine, fear or enjoy that involve your breasts?

Vagina/Vulva

- How old were you when you got your period and is there a particular moment around that time that stands out in your memory? Can you think of why it's exactly that moment that you remember?
- Do you know your vagina/vulva? How do you know it? What do you think about when you think about your "history" with your vagina/vulva?
- If you have given birth, had an abortion or miscarriage, in what way is this experience embedded in the emotional and muscle memory of your vagina?
- What's it like for you when you have your OB-GYN or midwife/nurse check-up? How is this "common" and "regular," typically annual event embedded in your experiential memory? Or, the first time. What was that like?
- Do you have memories of "discovering" your sexual organs? Exploring them? Realizing things about them?
- Do they feel transgressive to you? Why/how, or why not?
- What kind of emotional responses/experiences has this part of your body brought you in your life?

Penis/Testicles

- What's your earliest memory involving your penis/testicles?

- Do you remember the first time you noticed that someone else noticed your penis/testicles?
- Are you circumcised, or not, and whichever it is, do you have a memory of a time when this was an "issue" or something you or someone else reacted to it in a way that has created a memory for you?
- Has your penis ever gotten you "in trouble"?
- Do you have memories of "discovering" your sexual organs? Exploring them? Realizing things about them?
- Do they feel transgressive to you? Why/how, or why not?
- What kind of emotional responses/experiences has this part of your body brought you in your life?

Shaping your body part memory into a poem:

It may be that you have a specific body part memory that is painful or difficult for you to write about. Or perhaps you need the humor and levity that rhymes and rhythms invite. Sometimes writing prose in personal essay or memoir can feel as though it demands too much that all the words get in the way, that there is no room for silence or breath, where space and sparsity can carry or capture the meaning better for you. So you can try experimenting with poetry, like I have done in the "Vagina" chapter (see the poem "A Bloody Mess") and in the "Hips" chapter (see "Ode to My Hips").

Acknowledgements

It really does take a village. The writing about life through the lens of my body-parts started in 2018, when I was in my first semester at University of Southern Maine's Stonecoast MFA program. Thanks to the encouragement of "give me more like this" from my generous faculty mentor Suzanne Strempek Shea a thesis project was born, which eventually became the book you now hold in your hands. Careful readings, revisions, and much fine tuning took place during my final semester with my wise mentor Debra Marquart, and a rigorous developmental edit followed with Allison K. Williams, whose methodic and keenly practical literary eye taught me much. I feel lucky that my manuscript found its way to Alexis Paige, a once acquisitions editor at Vine Leaves Press, and that my voice and project resonated with her. Editor Melissa Slayton suggested important tweaks in the final round, for which I know the book is better. In the capable hands of Vine Leaves Press's publishing director Aime McCracken and publisher Jessica Bell, *Body: My Life in Parts* took shape and turned into something real, a dream realized, and joining the Vine Leaves Press author community has been such a wonderful bonus on this journey. I am also grateful to my diverse and supportive literary community which extends across several continents, both virtual and in person; the various robust Binders for writers on Facebook and the folks engaging with my Maine Writers Studio are just two examples. As a writer whose first language is not English, I have been hungry to develop and deepen my understanding of the English language and words in general (in many languages), and it is with my husband T.A. Perry, whose writing and publishing career is long and illustrious, that I have found a steady and inspirational companion in all things literary. His enthusiastic support of my creative life and endeavors is a true blessing. I am also thankful for my sister Tone and all my dear friends in Norway, the US, France, and Israel who have patiently and big-heartedly listened when I have read from or gabbed about my work-in-progress as they encouraged me to keep going. Finally, my three sons Tobias Thor, Gabriel Balder, and Benyamin Odin deserve a shout out as my premier cheerleading team, as well as my parents who have always encouraged me to be fearless and curious.

Excerpts from some chapters have been published in anthologies and literary magazines.

From "Vagina" chapter: "When Your Period is a Religious Affair," in *Stained: An Anthology of Writing About Menstruation*, Querencia Press, 2023.

From "Belly" chapter: "Belly," in *Awakenings: Writing on the Body and Consciousness*, ELJ Editions, 2023.

From "Skin" chapter: "Skin in the Game" in *Her Stry*, March 13, 2023.

From "Vagina" chapter: "Ink Stains and Blood Stains: The Spring of My Becoming," in *INK*, Hippocampus Books, 2022.

From "Breasts" chapter: "The Deep End" in *Dorothy Parker's Ashes*, March 15, 2021.

From "Heart" chapter: "The Making of the Viking Jewess", in *Lilith Magazine*, Winter, 2015-2016.

Vine Leaves Press

Enjoyed this book?
Go to *vineleavespress.com* to find more.
Subscribe to our newsletter: